DATE DUE

How to Make and Repair Your Own Fishing Tackle

Also by Jim Mayes
How to Make Your Own Knives

How to Make and Repair Your Own Fishing Tackle

An Illustrated
Step-by-Step Guide
for the Fisherman
and Hobbyist

Jim Mayes

Illustrated by Bill McKinley

Dodd, Mead & Company • New York

Copyright © 1986 by James H. Mayes, Jr.

Published by Dodd, Mead & Company, Inc.
79 Madison Avenue, New York, N.Y. 10016
Distributed in Canada by
McClelland and Stewart Limited, Toronto
Manufactured in the United States of America

Designed by Erich Hobbing

First Edition

Library of Congress Cataloging-in-Publication Data

Mayes, Jim.
How to make and repair your own fishing tackle.

1. Fishing tackle—Design and construction.
2. Fishing tackle—Maintenance and repair.   I. Title.
SH447.M38   1986   688.7'912   85-25226
ISBN 0-396-08555-5
ISBN 0-396-08610-1 (pbk.)

1 2 3 4 5 6 7 8 9 10

To friends and fellow members of
The Izaak Walton League of America . . .

whose dedicated conservation activities
for three-quarters of a century
have made America a better place
to live and fish.

Contents

Preface

Some of my best fishing buddies maintain that fishing doesn't begin until they have a denizen of the deep on the end of their line. I've got to admit that catching fish is fairly basic to this sport that more Americans (some 60 million of us) pursue than any other, so I'm a little reluctant to take exception.

Deep down, though, I can't help feeling a tad sorry for them. I think they're missing part of the fun, and a whole lot of the self-satisfaction, that go with catching fish on tackle and lures that are products of one's own creativity. From my perspective, another big advantage of an evening spent feathering a hook or wrapping a guide is the opportunity it affords to contemplate my next fishing trip.

Then there's that other reality of making and repairing your own tackle that's difficult to overlook: It saves a lot of hard-earned cash. Take a simple spinnerbait, for example. Even if you order yours in quantity from one of the catalog houses, you're going to have anywhere from one to two dollars invested in every lure you tie on your line. Yet once an initial investment has been made in a mold, components for an identical lure will cost you less than twenty-five cents. If you lose as many spinnerbaits as I do fishing stickups and structure, you're beginning to look at some pretty hefty savings over a season.

In recent years, there has been a proliferation—nay, an explosion—in the number and variety of lures, rods, reels, and other tackle available to fisherfolk. Some, I suspect, may catch more fishermen than fish. But at the same time, lots of the old, favorite lures many of us have tucked away in our tackle boxes are long since "out of print"; you can't find them on the shelves of any tackle shop. But as surely as another record-setting fish will be caught next spring, you can clone your favorite lure at your workbench with a little time, effort, and know-how.

When I was a kid, several fishing seasons ago, most casting rods were made of tubular steel. An old Heddon Pal still hangs in my rod rack, as good as the day it was bought some four decades back. But its action isn't in the same league with the fiberglass rods that came a few years later, and is not even roughly comparable with that of a modern graphite or boron shaft. Nor, unfortunately, is the cost. I paid fifty to eighty dollars for the store-bought graphite and boron rods I now own, but with them I can feel ol' Mr. Bass the moment he picks up on my plastic worm. Homemade boron and graphite rods cost about half as much as the ready-made models, yet offer the same advantages.

I regard my tackle-making activities in much the same light as I do the application of these endeavors: I fish and make tackle because both are relaxing and satisfying hobbies. The best part of it is that while tackle making and tackle using are eminently compatible pastimes, one seldom interferes with the other. Excepting emergency repairs (described in Chapter 11), tackle making is an indoor project done mostly when weather, closed season, or limited time prohibits a journey to lake or stream.

As you read this book, I believe you'll be pleasantly surprised at the modest investment required to get started on making your own tackle. Only the basic workshop tools are needed to make most lures, and virtually no tools at all are essential to rod building. Moreover, many of the tools and specialized workbench equipment you'll find helpful to tackle making can be made by any reasonably skilled home hobbyist. These tools and how to make them are described in appropriate places throughout the book.

As you order and begin going through catalogs published by companies specializing in tackle components (a list of reputable firms is included in the Appendix and discussed in Chapter 4), you'll discover the ready availability of almost every item you may want or need. If, for example, you decide to forgo carving your own plugs, you'll find that plastic bodies can be obtained at prices far below those of finished lures.

Or, to cite another example, say you're in love with your new graphite casting rod, but you really do wish it had a handle of cork rather than molded plastic. When you build your own rods, such wishes are readily transformed into reality. Or perhaps your old glass rod still meets your needs, but its guides are worn from years of use. No problem—order and install new ones made of aluminum oxide or whatever miracle of modern technology turns you on.

It's been said that writers write more for themselves than for their readers, and perhaps this is so. Certain it is that writers like to write about things they know and enjoy, and for people with whom they feel a kinship.

So it is with this book. I have written it for people who, like myself, are both fishermen and home hobbyists; people who have some ability with tools and like to express themselves; and finally, people who are totally lacking in any deep-seated motivation to spend more than they have to for custom-made fishing tackle.

I hope you are one of these people. If you are, I believe you will read and enjoy this book as much as I have enjoyed writing it.

How to Make and Repair Your Own Fishing Tackle

1. A Brief History of Fishing Tackle

Way back in 1653 when old Ike Walton wrote that little book that made him famous, *The Compleat Angler or The Contemplative Man's Recreation,* he simply formalized as a sport a pursuit that is one of man's oldest occupations. Fishhooks made of bone and bronze have been unearthed in association with ancient man, and who can forget the numerous biblical references to fishing?

Walton, the patron saint of sport fishing, took trout from English chalk streams with an eighteen-foot wooden rod, line made of braided horsehair, and hooks dressed with bucktail and other natural hair. Even though the old fellow also had an unfortunate penchant for live bait (now illegal in most of the streams he fished), you've got to give him credit for perseverance and fortitude. I doubt that many of us today would be devotees of angling were we required to use the tools at his disposal. His formula for making horsehair fishing line, for example, went like this:

> First, let your hair be clean-washed ere you go about to twist it, and then choose not only the cleanest hair for it, but hairs that be of equal bigness, for such do usually stretch all together and break all together, which hairs of an unequal bigness never do, but break singly, and so deceive the angler who trusts them.

Without ever coming up for air, Ike went on to describe how the horsehair should be "wetted in water," then twisted again, and so on. Fortunately, the way Walton fished, he needed only about twelve feet of line. Had he been making thirty-yard casts the way some of us do today, I suspect we fishermen would have had to look elsewhere for a patron saint; poor old Izaak would have been so busy braiding horsehair that he'd never have gotten around to writing *The Compleat Angler.*

Ancient anglers, in common with those of Walton's seventeenth century England, apparently fished also with a tight (as opposed to a running) line. I find it a little puzzling that folks as inventive as the ancient Greeks and Romans, to whom we're indebted for the earliest written accounts of sport fishing, never tumbled to the advantages of extra line. But, strangely enough, all evidence indicates that for thousands of years the fastening of a relatively short line to the end of a rod was accepted practice.

Equally strange, the fishing reel doesn't make its appearance in angling literature until the middle of the seventeenth century, and it waited even longer for general acceptance.

The problem of tracing the history of fishing gear, of course, is that Man learned to fish a long, long time before he learned to write. Even if we assume that the first fish story was told about an hour after the first angler caught his first fish, it was quite a spell before the first outdoor writer came along.

Although most of our knowledge of early fishing tackle and techniques has been passed along to us by the ancient Greeks and Romans, archaeological evidence suggests that the Chinese and Egyptians were using essentially the same equipment centuries before them. The earliest known representation of fishing with rod, line, and hook are figures painted on Egyptian tombs dating from about 2000 B.C. One such painting, from the Tomb of Ti, shows a man catching what appears to be a catfish, using a long pole and short line.

Hooks used by Egyptians of the first dynasty were barbless and made of copper, but by the eighteenth dynasty, barbed hooks made of bronze were being used. Ancient bronze, an alloy of tin and copper, was substantially harder than metals previously used and could be worked very fine. This quality no doubt endeared it to ancient anglers, both for live-bait fishing and for tying artificial flies.

The first extensive written account of angling as a sport dates from the third century, when a Roman nature writer named Claudius Aelianus described fly-fishing for trout ("the fish with a speckled skin") on a Macedonian river. Aelianus, who may well have been the first outdoor writer, told also of fishing for grayling, which he called thyme-fish, in the river Tecinus in northern Italy, and some historians believe that salmon were caught on artificial flies in England during Roman times.

Several hundred years before Aelianus attempted to popularize sport fishing, Plato wrote of it in a somewhat different light. Recognizing that not all fishing is angling, which he defined as taking fish with rod, hook, and line, Plato implied that it was an unworthy temptation that took young men's minds from the eminently more worthwhile pursuit of making war. It's hard to argue, even today, that if more people spent more time making tackle and using it, there wouldn't be as much time to wage war.

Evidently, by the time Aelianus wrote, angling had come to be held in somewhat higher regard, because his account tells of using horsehair and twisted flax for making fishing line, and of using died wool, various feathers, wild boar's bristles, bronze, and lead for making lures. A reading of Aelianus's work suggests that he regarded such materials for making artificial lures as basic to the ordinary fisherman's tackle box (which, unfortunately, he neglected to describe).

Of all ancient tackle, it is perhaps the use and composition of the angler's rod that is most heavily shrouded in the mists of an uncertain past. It seems fairly certain that it was of one-piece construction for many centuries, although its length and weight appear to have varied considerably. Light rods in ancient Greece and Rome were made of a reed known botanically as *Arundo domax*, sometimes called the "bamboo of Europe." Early Egyptian rods almost certainly were made from similar reeds that grew along the Nile, and we can assume that the ancient Chinese were familiar with the attributes of bamboo.

Stronger and more powerful rods were made of cornel wood (referred to by Aelianus), which was similar to (and possibly the same as) the greenheart wood used extensively by European and American rod makers in the late nineteenth and early twentieth centuries. Unlike the magnum rod used by Izaak Walton, the rods used by ancient Greeks and Romans probably averaged six to eight feet in length. The line was of approximately the same length.

Although the use of braided horsehair (and, to a lesser extent, woven or twisted flax) dominated the European scene for hundreds of years, the ancient Chinese are believed to have used silk for their fishing lines at least as early as the fourth century B.C. The following description, literally translated, appeared in Chinese writings of that long-ago era: "By making a line of cocoon silk, a hook from a sharp needle, a rod from the branch of a bramble or dwarf bamboo, and using a grain of cooked rice as bait, one can be assured of catching a whole cartload of fish." It was also written that Emperor Wu of the Han Dynasty fished with "line of the finest white silk, a hook of pure gold, and a red carp [small goldfish] for bait."

It's impossible, for lack of records, to know the status of sport fishing and tackle development during the Dark Ages and following Renaissance period, but from the similarity between equipment described by Aelianus in the third century and Izaak Walton in the seventeenth, it's obvious that few momentous changes occurred. Indeed, wooden rods not too different from Walton's, line made of braided silk, and reels suited only for line storage were still being used by our grandfathers. Only in this century—and particularly in the past thirty or forty years—have major innovations been made in fishing tackle.

After enduring for centuries without major modification, the golden age of the wooden rod was relatively short-lived, actually lasting only from the late eighteenth century to about the middle of the nineteenth. During that period, and especially in the 1830s and 1840s, anonymous American craftsmen were turning out wooden rods that were beautifully executed in a variety of domestic and imported woods. Ash and hazel were popular woods for butt sections, and lancewood and greenheart were woods of preference for tips and midsections. Fittings of German and even sterling silver adorned many of these fine old rods, which were among the most beautiful ever made in America.

The demise of the wooden rod came gradually in the United States and took even longer in England and Europe, where tradition dies harder. Excellent wooden rods still were being sold in the early 1900s, and venerable specimens still could be seen on our lakes and rivers through the Depression years.

Following their commercial introduction in the 1860s, first in England and shortly after in the United States, the superiority of split-bamboo rods was generally acknowledged by the angling fraternity—fly fishermen and bait casters alike. Craftsmen such as Hiram Leonard, Charles Orvis, William Mitchell, and Robert Welch—known already

3

for their skill with wood—made the transition to bamboo with little difficulty. Others, perhaps less flexible or more traditional, continued to supply the declining market for wooden rods until it vanished altogether.

A gentleman named Charles Murphy of Newark, New Jersey, is credited with making and marketing the first commercial six-strip split-bamboo rods here in America. Some of his early work is on display at the Museum of American Fly Fishing in Manchester, Vermont. It was Hiram Leonard, a wilderness merchant and gunsmith from Bangor, Maine, however, who perfected commercial manufacture of the modern hexagonal split-bamboo fly rod. Many of the craftsmen he hired—names like Ed Payne, Tom Chubb, Fred Thomas, and George Varney come to mind—went on to become famous rod makers in their own right.

By the turn of the century, rod builders were using direct flame or kilns to temper split bamboo to the springiness of coiled steel. As this and other innovations were producing faster-action rods, complementary changes were taking place in lines and reels.

Fishing reels had come into general use in England around 1700 and in the United States by 1750. These early reels were simple wooden spools on metal or wood carriages. The first edition of Ike Walton's *Compleat Angler*, published in 1653, made no mention of reels, but the second edition, published four years later, speaks of a "wheel" used by certain salmon fishermen. (It's quite likely that the ancient Chinese used reels of some type centuries earlier.)

The first American click reel on record was made by J. L. Sage of Frankfort, Kentucky, in 1848. In 1874, Charlie Orvis patented a narrow-spooled, ventilated fly-casting reel that became the prototype of multiplier reels to follow. Orvis's reel was also the first to be mounted beneath the rod grip rather than on the side, thereby improving the balance of the rod and significantly embellishing precision casting.

Even as these important developments were occurring in the world of fly-fishing, equally profound happenings were stirring among bait casters. As a classic form of sport fishing, bait casting evolved more slowly than did fly-fishing. During the halcyon years of the nineteenth and early twentieth centuries, when fly-fishing was becoming known as the sport of kings and presidents, bait casting was restricted largely to the bays and backwaters of the South, where the warm waters couldn't support the noble trout.

Things had taken a decided turn for the better in 1810 when a Kentucky watchmaker named George Snyder produced the first bait-casting reel. His invention, which predated the first effective fly-fishing reel, was inspired by the needs of his fellow local fishermen, who used long cane poles with light tips to flip minnows to largemouth bass. Before Snyder's invention, bait casters simply tied their lines to the ends of their rods, just as Walton had done two centuries earlier.

But even after Snyder's reel gave southern anglers the opportunity to fight the heavy-bodied largemouths with running line, the sport languished in most parts of America and was no factor at all in England. At a time when such geniuses as Theodore Gordon were inspiring writers (and even poets) with their realistic insect imitations designed to entice trout, bait casters were seemingly content to toss their worms, minnows, and cutbait from banks and johnboats.

To compound the problem, early-day makers of bait-casting lures were poorly rewarded for their efforts. Silk line, even when improved, was poorly suited to long-distance bait casting, and reels lacked level-winding mechanisms for returning retrieved line evenly onto the reel spool until well into the twentieth century. Many a would-be young bait caster (I was among them) gave up in disgust after suffering his ninth backlash in ten casts. Fly-fishing, it appeared, would remain forever the realm of the serious angler.

Remnants of the author's first tackle (cigar) box, some of which continue to produce fish. The Acme "trout reel" was sold by Sears, Roebuck & Company in 1902 for ten cents. A top-of-the-line Pennell reel sold that year for three dollars.

Then, beginning shortly after World War II, a series of wonderfully synergistic events occurred that would make fishing the most popular participatory sport in America. It's difficult, perhaps impossible, to chronicle precisely the course of these events, as numerous developments—some successful, others destined for failure—were taking place more or less simultaneously.

Almost certainly, though, we can point to the wartime invention of nylon, which led to the introduction in 1946 of braided nylon fishing line, as a watershed event. A few years later, further experiments led to the development of the now-familiar and universally used monofilament line. Although the first monoline exhibited a monumental stretch capacity of 20 to 25 percent, its introduction made spinning and spin-casting reels a commercial reality—and fishermen out of 60 million Americans!

Actually, the concept behind spinning and spin-casting reels—concentric coils of line flowing off a fixed or nonrevolving spool—is neither recent nor complex. The first practical spinning reel was invented in 1905 by an Englishman named Alfred Holden, who was inspired no doubt by the bobbins used in his family's cotton mills. The first spinning reel marketed in the United States was a French model designed by Paul

5

Mauborgne. But, due largely to the unavailability of a suitable line, so few were sold that fixed-spool reels remained unknown to most Americans.

With the perfection of monofilament line in the late 1940s, the sport of spin fishing took off like a scalded dog. Thousands of Americans who had been intimidated by fly-fishing and bait casting invested in spinning equipment and took to lakes and streams. Dozens of spinning reels with foreign accents—notably French, German, and Italian—made their appearance in American tackle shops. The most successful were the French-made Mitchells, introduced to American fishermen by the New York import house of Charles Garcia.

By the early 1950s, most American tackle makers had smelled the bacon and introduced spinning reels of their own manufacture. Yet, despite the availability of monofilament line from DuPont and others, no wholly satisfactory rod-making material was yet available. After a century of producing increasingly expensive split-bamboo fly rods and wooden and tubular-steel casting rods designed to handle ⅝-ounce plugs, no one quite had the formula for making cheap and efficient rods able to handle the ⅛-ounce lures that spinning equipment cast most effectively.

Rod blanks designed for heavy fly-fishing provided one answer, and a lot of us who'd never wrapped a rod in our lives began stripping the guides from venerable flyrods and replacing them with larger guides suitable for spinning. The first spinning rod I really felt comfortable with was an ancient 7½-foot tubular-steel fly rod fitted with a new reel seat and big guides. I still think of it as one of the best smallmouth sticks I ever owned.

Commercial rod makers kept casting about for an answer, and finally found it in resin-impregnated fiberglass. The early models, in common with split bamboo, tended to take on a permanent set if you left them leaning in the corner too long, and there were problems with splintering. But after a few years of experimentation, the rod makers—led, I believe, by Shakespeare—worked out most of the technical bugs, and good, economical spinning tackle had come of age.

The event that really turned America, and especially American kids, into a nation of fishermen, though, was the introduction of the closed-face, or spin-casting, reel. One company, a Tulsa-based firm with the unlikely name of Zero Hour Bomb Company (later Zebco), was almost single-handedly responsible. Until 1949, Zebco's only product was an electrically detonated time bomb for oil-well shooting. But in June of that year, a job applicant named R. D. Hull appeared on their doorstep with a strange-looking contraption that folks came to call a "beer can with a hole in both ends." The first closed-face spinning reel was introduced experimentally about a year later, and by 1954 Zebco's Model 33 had become, by nearly everyone's admission, America's favorite reel. The ultimate in simplicity, the Zebco 33 (and, later, a cheaper "youth" model) made fishermen of kids and experts of tyros.

Today, three decades later, spinning tackle of one kind or another remains by far the most popular fishing gear sold in America. Spin casting alone accounts for about 45 percent of all freshwater tackle sold, and straight spinning outfits account for another 35 percent of the market. Bait-casting tackle, despite the unfortunate holdover of its name (today it is used almost exclusively with artificial lures) comprises about 15 percent of sales, and fly-fishing—once the domain of every dedicated angler—now accounts for only 5 percent of sales.

Today's anglers are indeed a blessed breed. Millions of kids and young adults begin fishing today without a hint of the travail their elders once suffered in the name of angling. These converts, far from overcrowding our lakes and rivers, have brought with them the funds and expert attention required to create a vastly improved fishing environment for all of us who enjoy the great out-of-doors.

An equally fortunate offshoot of the boom in fishing's popularity has been the multiplying availability of rod and tackle components for those of us sufficiently enamored of our sport to want something a little out of the ordinary—something we've made with our own hands. Even in the days of the great fly-rod makers of the past century, tackle making was never a craft plied by men of ordinary means and talents. Today, thank goodness, all that has changed profoundly.

2. Tackle Terms: How to Find Your Way

In common with just about every human endeavor that involves specialized skills and knowledge, fishing has a language all its own. Of course every school kid knows a fishhook or rod and reel when he (or, increasingly these days, she) sees it. However, not all fishermen, and practically no laymen at all, are able to recite the names and functions of all the specialized parts and components that can be found in any well-equipped tackle box. Nor, for that matter, should they be able to. After all, I've driven a car for years, and still would be hard pressed to tell you whether a sun gear fits on the drive shaft or starter motor. Point is, you don't have to know tackle to catch fish.

But things get a little different when you decide you want to *make* your own tackle as well as use it. All of a sudden you're playing in a different sandlot—one where knowing and specifying the right part and size for just the purpose you have in mind can make a big difference in how well your project turns out. I can't tell you how to build a car, but I think I can help you have some fun and save some bucks making your own tackle.

As we go along together through this book, we'll be talking about some components and tools that serve only a single purpose. These, for the most part, will be introduced and described at appropriate places in the chapters that follow, and there's also a glossary in the back of the book. What I'd like to do right now is get you well enough acquainted with the world of fishing tackle so that you'll feel comfortable discussing your needs and problems with friends and suppliers with whom you'll be talking and to whom you'll be writing.

There's nothing very complicated about a rod. It has a handle you hold on to and an end where the line comes off, doesn't it? Well, yes and no. In between, it gets a tad more complicated than that. Some of the parts you never worried about before you'll want to shake hands with, now that you've decided to become a rod builder.

Take the handle, for example. Its parts, in most constructions, include a butt grip you hold on to, a reel seat that holds the reel, and a foregrip that fits in front of the reel seat. In most constructions it also

RODS

has a butt cap that protects the butt grip and keeps dirt out.

Depending on purpose, handles may be one-handed or two-handed, straight or pistol-grip, cork or soft (resilient) plastic, unitary or multiple-piece construction.

Rod shafts (called blanks) are today composed of three materials: fiberglass, graphite, and boron. But there's no such thing as a 100 percent boron rod, and some of the best graphite rods being made still have fiberglass in them. The chapter on rod building will discuss the characteristics (both good and bad) of each material.

Aligned along the spine of the rod blank are guides that direct the line along the curvature of the rod as it is flexed in casting and fighting fish. Today there are more than half a dozen materials used for making guides. Some are decidedly better than others, but some—in my opinion—aren't worth the extra cost. These, too, are described in Chapter 5, which I strongly recommend you read before sitting down to order parts.

LURES

In the chapters that follow, we'll be talking about making your own jigs, spoons, plugs, spinnerbaits, plastic worms, and sundry other artificial devices we hope will ring the dinner bell for whatever species of fish we're after. Some lures, notably those cast from lead, require little more to make than the proper equipment. Casting plugs made from wood, on the other hand, require little in the way of equipment, but a lot in the way of effort as you test, tune, and improve them.

Even the lures we make at home require hardware such as hooks, split rings, screw eyes, and clevises, which no home craftsman is capable of making. These small but important items must be ordered in several sizes and configurations, else you'll find yourself in the middle of a project with no way to complete it until some additional component is obtained. The price of having an adequate supply of lure components on hand is small when measured against the frustration of not having what you need when you need it.

HOOKS

When you consider that there are about fifty thousand different sizes, styles, and finishes of hooks, it's obvious that not everyone agrees on the relative merits of each. The hooks discussed and recommended in this book are those I've found best suited to the use cited. In most instances, though, another style or size may work equally well or even better, and I hope you'll experiment as you go along.

In ordering hooks, you should know that no universal standards exist when it comes to size. Each pattern tends to be a little different, and manufacturers establish their own guidelines. Numbering systems are useful only for comparing sizes within a given pattern. In a given pattern, the higher the number, the smaller the hook. When the size reaches 1, however, the numerical system is reversed and a zero is added. The illustrations of a few selected hook patterns I've included in the Appendix will give you an idea of relative sizes.

In ordering double and treble hooks to hang from your plugs and spoons, I suggest that you select bronze-plated ones in sizes 2, 4, 6, and 8 (largest to smallest). For safety-pin spinnerbaits and buzzbaits you'll want O'Shaughnessy long-shank hooks in sizes 2/0 and 3/0, and for jig making you'll need O'Shaughnessy or Aberdeen jig hooks in sizes 2/0, 3/0, and 4/0. For years I've gone with Southern Sproats in sizes 2/0, 3/0, and 4/0 for use with plastic worms, but of late I've been impressed with the so-called "Keeper" hooks from Mr. Twister in the same sizes. I remain unimpressed with the worm hooks having built-in kinks in their shanks; logic tells me they're inherently weaker than straight shanks.

Swivels, clevises, screw eyes, and split rings are among the other lure-making components you'll want to order in some quantity. The main problem you're likely to encounter is keeping their size designations straight in your head; I've been ordering the darn things for years and still have trouble. Be sure to check the catalogs closely.

OTHER LURE COMPONENTS

In lure making, your primary use of swivels (not swivel snaps) will be for making spinnerbaits. Swivels are numbered like hooks, with the larger numbers up to 0 designating smaller size. Swivels are made in sizes as small as 16 and as large as 5/0, though I've never found an application for either. I think it likely that sizes 5 through 9 (largest to smallest) will satisfy most any need you may have. Should the catalog house you order from lack one of these sizes, go up or down a number. There's no question that the Sampo brand of ball-bearing swivels are the best made, but at a significantly higher cost. To me, they're not that much better than ordinary barrel swivels, but this is a decision you'll have to make for yourself after checking prices.

Of the two types of clevises in general use, stirrup and folded, I tend to favor the former because I believe they give more freedom to the spinner blades. This is purely a personal choice, which, I feel it fair to mention, the Mepps people don't share with me. They've managed to sell millions of spinnerbaits fitted with folded clevises. The numbering system used for clevises makes a little more sense, with higher numbers indicating larger sizes. In my experience, sizes 1 through 4 will satisfy 99 percent of your needs. The best ones I've used are made of nickel-plated brass: they don't tend to corrode like the brass ones sometimes do.

Screw eyes should be ordered in sizes 4 through 8 (smallest to largest) in both open and closed configurations. The sizes of these gadgets vary not only in the diameter of their eyes, but also in the length of their shanks. You'll need open eyes for those times you want to hang the hook directly from the screw eye rather than from an intermediate split ring.

Split rings, which you'll use for hook hangers and line ties, are available in sizes 1 through 5, with 1 being the smallest. You may never find a use for the largest and smallest sizes, but the cost is so inconsequential that I advise ordering a few dozen in all five sizes.

Other lure-making components, each of which are covered in appropriate chapters, include beads, spinner blades, stainless-steel leader wire, connector springs, delta blades, and a variety of hair, feathers, tinsel, and other dressing. Ordering such components is a fairly straightforward affair that requires no great decision making other than deciding what you want to use.

Chapter 4, on ordering tackle-making components, deals more extensively with catalog houses, and addresses and phone numbers are listed in Appendix B. As your first move, even before you thumb your way through the pages of this book, let me urge you to take pen in hand and to send for every catalog listed. Several offer helpful hints I may have overlooked. And, if nothing else, they're the darndest "wish" books you'll ever find.

3. Setting Up Your Workbench

Tackle making and repair has been done in every location from stream bank and boat deck to library tables and kitchen counter top. Nothing wrong with that. When you get serious about tackle making, though, I think you're going to find that nothing will quite substitute for a small workbench that's more or less dedicated to that and not much else.

Like most tinkerers and home hobbyists, one of the first things I did when the little woman and I bought the ol' homestead was set up a big (eight-foot), heavy (two-by-two construction) bench in one corner of the basement. Just about every repair that's been made around Mayes Manor since that time has been pretty closely associated with that workbench and the pegboard of tools that hangs over it.

For a good many years after I started repairing, and later making, fishing tackle at home, my venerable old bench served the purpose fairly well. Only thing was, I got to noticing that more and more bench-top space was being chewed up by tackle components, and less and less was available for hand loading, knife making, leatherwork, and a few of the other things I like to dabble at from time to time. Worse yet, it got to where the wife was afraid to go near the thing, it looked so spooky (*she* said).

Finally, I did what I should have done long before: I went over to our friendly Hines lumberyard and loaded the pickup with thirty dollars' worth of ¾-inch plywood and a few 8-foot lengths of two-by-fours. Half a morning's work produced a serviceable bench, which measures 28 by 64 inches and stands 40 inches high. It sits over in the corner of the basement also occupied by the big bench—one runs along the east-west wall and the other along the north-south wall.

Eighty, maybe 90 percent of the tools I use for tackle making hang on a pegboard over my larger, general-purpose bench. Only the specialized tools and components used for tackle tinkering are allowed on the tackle bench. I can't say I do any better work, but at least I'm organized.

Organization, I'm persuaded, is the big secret to being an efficient tackle maker. Lure making, in particular, requires literally scores of small items, from clevises and hollow beads to spinner blades and hook assortments. I must have accumulated twenty or thirty different sizes and

This workbench, the construction of which is described in the text, is used by the author for most of his tackle making.

colors of spinner blades alone. Being able to locate what you need when you need it is what keeps tacklesmiths happy and reasonably sane.

Years ago, I kept all my tackle-making components in lure boxes and the little plastic boxes a lot of them come in; I even recycled matchboxes for the purpose. Then one day I happened to notice how neatly the wife had all her sewing supplies tucked away in a couple of those little plastic storage-organizer boxes. Now, a couple of the fifteen-drawer cabinets and a couple more of the thirty-drawer jobs sit across the back of my bench. I use the little self-adhesive file folder labels on the front of each drawer to identify its contents.

Multiple-drawer storage-organizers (available at most hardware stores) are great for keeping track of tackle-making components. Small plastic bins (top and foreground) keep hooks and other frequently used items readily accessible. Gummed labels identify various items by type and size.

Drawer-filled storage-organizers work great for just about every small tackle-making component except hooks. They're a problem all to themselves because, as every fisherman knows, they possess an infernal ability to ball themselves up in unbelievable tangles that no amount of shaking can unravel. The best answer I've found for hook storage are little (four-by-five-inch) plastic bins that stack separately or lock together with a special strip that's supplied. They can be fixed to the wall or (as I've done) simply arranged across the back of the workbench. I found them at the same builders' supply store where I got the storage-organizers; maybe you can, too.

Keep your eyes open, also, for those plastic inserts used by packagers to arrange and display cheese samplers and similar delicacies. It seems that a few of them always turn up around our house at Christmastime. These, and plastic egg cartons, are great for temporary storage of parts when you're building spinnerbaits or repairing a reel. Especially when disassembling reels, I number the individual slots of egg cartons so the reel goes back together in the same order it came apart. This prevents the embarrassment of getting a reel reassembled and discovering a couple of leftover parts.

Once you've got your workbench set up in a fashion you feel comfortable with, take a close look at the general-purpose tools you already have. Then decide what special-purpose tools you're going to need for tackle making. As noted earlier, most do-it-yourselfers will already have many of the tools required, and others can be improvised. Specialized tools and devices, such as plaster molds for jig making, are discussed in chapters devoted to that particular endeavor.

Commonly Used Workbench Tools

Among the specialized tools the home tackle maker will likely make for himself are (top to bottom) a wire-bending device, a wooden-handled spoon for stirring heated plastic, a long-handled clamp for holding lures while painting, a wooden mold or anvil for making spoons, and tools for putting eyes on lures.

Not every tacklesmith gets into all aspects of the hobby; some, for example, mold a lot of jigs and spinnerbaits, but seldom if ever make their own worms or plugs. Others may be interested only in building their own customized rods. This is something you want to keep in mind as you review the tool list I've put together. Remember, too, that tackle

PLIERS

making isn't exactly a strong-arm hobby, and many of the tools used in its pursuit tend to be on the diminutive side.

Whether you intend to specialize, or go whole hog and stock your entire tackle box with items you've made, pliers of several varieties will find a welcome place on your workbench.

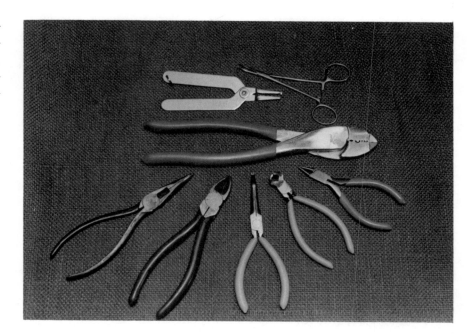

Specialized pliers that will be used by the tackle maker include (left to right, top to bottom) split-ring pliers, forceps, a crimping tool, sharp-nosed pliers, diagonal cutters, bent flat-nose pliers, end cutters, and tapered round-nose pliers.

I can't remember exactly where it was, but several years ago I found a set of small pliers (four to six inches long) that have proved themselves a thousand times in making tackle. They consist of tapered round-nose, end-cutters, bent flat-nose, and diagonal-cutters. If you can find a set like this, I urge you to buy it; you'll use these pliers for all sorts of wire bending and fitting chores.

The relatively heavy-gauge (.040–.050) stainless-steel wire used in making the shafts of safety-pin spinnerbaits is tough to cut. For the purpose, you'll need a pair of heavy electrician's pliers or, better yet, a pair of leveraged cutters. (A word of caution: Heavy-gauge wire jumps like crazy when you cut it; for safety's sake, cover it with a towel or wiping cloth when cutting.)

Another tool I use all the time for several assignments is a small pair of locking (vise grip) pliers. In the sharp-nose configuration, they make a dandy vise for dressing jigs. Used in this manner, they must be fixed to the bench with one of the mounting brackets that frequently accompany them.

Heavy-duty crimping pliers, such as those sold by Cabela's and other suppliers, are of more limited use, but mighty handy when you need to crimp leader sleeves. They're also tough enough to cut spinnerbait wire. One little tool that will go a long way toward reducing your frustration level is a pair of split-ring pliers. Worth Tackle Company makes a pair that sells for just over a dollar, or you can get a fancier pair for about six bucks.

Regular tin snips will get you through a piece of light-gauge steel or aluminum, but if you plan to work with anything thicker than about 20 gauge, you'll need a set of compound-leverage (aviation) snips. The problem with these is that three are needed—one to cut straight and one each to cut right-hand and left-hand curves. Unless you plan to make a lot of your own spoons, these are something you can live without.

The flat-blade screwdrivers you have in your tool kit or on your workbench will suffice for most, but not all, tackle-making chores. For affixing hook hangers to plugs and for working on reels, you should invest in a set of jeweler's or miniature precision screwdrivers. The imported jobs work fine for lures, but I advise the slightly more expensive American-made sets for reel repair. Also handy for working on some reels are the miniature precision nut-driver sets. The only problem here is that, with so many imported reels on the market, you need sets in both metric and fractional-inch configurations. Both are available at hobby and electronics shops.

SCREWDRIVERS

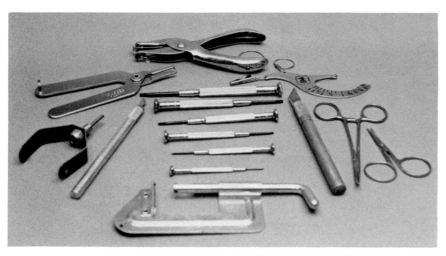

Small workbench tools that will prove handy for special assignments include (from the top) a paper punch, postal scale, forceps and fly-tying scissors, a wire-bending tool by Worth, precision screwdrivers, X-acto knives, a winding thread bobbin, and split-ring pliers.

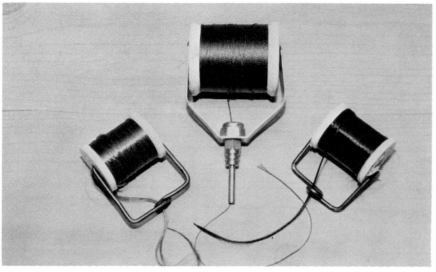

Bobbins, used for winding thread on jigs and other lures, can be purchased (center) or simply made from coat-hanger wire.

 Chances are your workbench already houses all the saws you'll ever really need for making tackle: hacksaw, coping saw, and backsaw. The latter two will come in handy for cutting and trimming the wood blocks used in plug making, while the hacksaw will prove useful in cutting Plexiglas for diving lips and heavy-gauge metal for spoons. I also use my hacksaw for cutting big chunks of lead down to sizes that will fit in my melting furnace.

HAMMERS
 I can't think of anything you'll use hammers for except forming spoons. For this purpose, you'll need a soft-faced (rubber-tipped) peening hammer for making smooth-finished spoons and a regular eight-ounce ball peen hammer for making hammered-finish spoons. In Chapter 10 I'll suggest a cheap method of making a soft-faced hammer that works well.

This soft-faced (rubber-tipped) hammer is used for forming smooth-finished spoons. As described in Chapter 10, it can be made cheaply by grinding down the peen of an 8-oz. ball peen hammer.

FILES AND RASPS
 Every tackle box should contain a small (needle) file for honing hooks, and your workbench may already hold several types. If you don't already have a set, I suggest that you hie yourself over to a hobby shop and pick up a few in various configurations, namely, flat, triangular, and round. You'll use them for a variety of tackle-making jobs. Other than needle

This selection of small files and rasps will be used by the tackle maker for several purposes. From left: Half-moon rasp, flat needle file, round needle rasp, rat-tail rasp, triangular needle file, rat-tail file, smooth-sided needle file, and 6-inch mill bastard file.

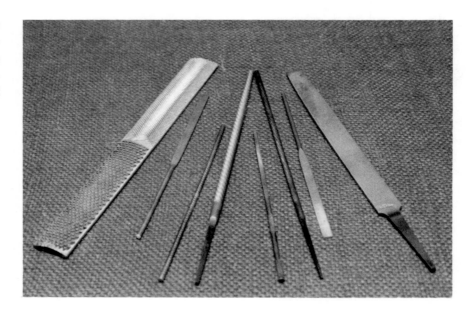

18

files, all you'll need is a regular flat or bastard file. The smaller sizes work best for lure making.

Two kinds of rasps are helpful, if not absolutely essential, for tackle making. The standard half-moon rasp with teeth sized for rough and finish work is used for roughing out wooden plugs and rod handles made of cork. A rat-tail rasp is necessary for sizing the inside diameters of cork rings and formed handles used in rod making.

Whenever you use files, of whatever persuasion, keep them working for you by cleaning them periodically with a file cleaner or wire brush. A wire wheel on a bench-mounted electric drill is fast and effective, especially for cleaning rasps.

Electric drills are amazingly cheap these days, and nearly every household has one. Drilling holes in lures is mostly precision work, hence an additional modest investment in one of the little presses designed to hold electric drills is money well spent. As for bits, the smaller-size ones (1/16 to 1/8 inch) are about all you'll ever find application for. Your local hardware store may be better stocked than mine, but I've found that I must go to a hobby shop for drill bits smaller than 1/16 inch. If you are working with small plugs (hence, small screw eyes), you will need two or three of the small, numbered bits.

DRILLS

Being as how one of the reasons for making your own tackle is to save money, it obviously isn't prudent to invest in power equipment just for tackle making. If, on the other hand, you've been considering investing in a bench-mounted belt sander or a small band saw, you'll find both are real time-savers when making lures and other tackle. My workshop has neither (maybe someday), but I frequently use a homemade sander that consists of an old fan motor belted to an arbor sold by Sears for about ten dollars. The arbor mounts a small drum sander on one side and flapper-type sander on the other. It saves an awful lot of hand sanding when making plugs.

OTHER POWER TOOLS

I also use a Dremel Moto-Tool for a variety of tackle-making tasks, including drilling 1/16-inch and smaller holes for screw eyes and such. The Moto-Tool kit comes with a number of small sanding discs, cutting heads, and other gadgets, nearly all of which can be used for tackle crafting at one time or another.

You're going to find as you go along that several small-tool items can make your job a lot quicker and easier. For example, I have a set of small wood gouges that are most helpful for carving the concave faces of chugger-type plugs (see Chapter 9) and for scooping out wooden molds or patterns used for making spoons (see Chapter 10). I feel more comfortable with my old Buck pocketknife, but the wood-carving set made by X-acto works wonderfully well for whittling plugs. A pair of small scissors, such as those used by fly tiers, is a real help for cutting thread, trimming hair, and assorted tasks associated with dressing jigs and treble hooks.

MISCELLANEOUS TOOLS

A small awl or ice pick is handy for starting drill holes in wood and plastic, and a center punch is just about indispensable for starting drill holes in metal spoons. A pick made from a large needle stuck in a small dowel is helpful for getting the tangles out of mylar and tinsel jig dressings, and for straightening out unevenly spaced rod wrappings.

I find myself continually using a small precision-dial caliper for checking and transferring measurements. If you get one, be sure that it measures accurately down to the nearest hundredth of an inch. A commercially made wire former, or one you make yourself, is essential for making spinnerbaits and wire leaders. Check Chapter 7 for a detailed discussion of wire-forming techniques.

Finally, if you're planning to mold lead heads for jigs or spinnerbaits, you will require a means of melting and molding lead. Chapter 6 deals with this aspect of tackle tinkering.

For heaven's sake, don't think for one minute that you need everything discussed here to get started making tackle. Hardly anyone I know has undertaken all aspects of tackle making at one time, nor should you try to. Although it's a billion-dollar business, tackle making is also a fun hobby. Take it a step at a time, don't get yourself overcommitted either timewise or financially, and enjoy. That's what this book is all about.

4. Ordering Tackle Components and Supplies

Now that Chapter 2 on tackle terminology and Chapter 3 on setting up your workbench have gotten you mentally prepared for it, let's talk a few minutes about the next step in our adventure—ordering the parts and supplies you'll be working with. We could call this chapter "learning to live with catalog houses and loving it," because that's going to be the thrust of our discussion.

In the chapters that follow, we'll be talking about tackle-making components, specialized tools, devices you can make or order, and how to put things together in proper sequence. However, a lot of the doing involves planning ahead so that you have what you need when you need it. So here are some suggestions on how to avoid the frustrations and pitfalls of dealing with people you'll likely never meet.

Not all fishermen are so blessed, but I happen to live only a couple of miles from one of the best tackle shops in the Midwest—Ed Shirley & Sons of Markham, Illinois. Ed and his boys are all sport fishermen and know the products they sell. I love tackle shops, and Ed's gotten enough of my bucks over the years to buy Mama a mink. (That's no problem in my case; Mama's one of my best fishing buddies.)

But tackle shops, no matter how good they are, cater primarily to folks that want to go fishing *right now*. Very few of them offer the variety—or the price—on tackle-making components that the specialized catalog houses are able to provide.

By far the best way to deal with catalog houses, once you've written to obtain their catalogs, is by phone. Many of them have an 800 number to facilitate this very thing. There are two big advantages to doing business by phone: First, you get your supplies a lot quicker—mailed or shipped UPS the same day in many instances; second, phoned orders give you the opportunity to discuss the project you're planning with an expert who has been through the routine many times. Let me cite an example. There's nothing quite as intimidating as opening a rod-component catalog for the first time and poring over the almost unbelievable variety of rod blanks, guides, handle material, wrapping thread, varnish, and all the rest. *You* know what you want your custom-built rod to do, but making all the right choices as to action, length, composi-

21

tion, appropriate guides, and so forth can be an imposing undertaking. When you call, the fellow on the other end of the line can be a mighty comforting influence, and will likely suggest some little item you'd never have thought of on your own. This book will help, but I'll never be able to cover every situation you'll encounter. Order takers at the better catalog houses do it every day.

No matter what section of the nation you live in, there will be a catalog house in your area that specializes in tackle-making components, tools, and supplies.

Now there's a devil in everybody's paradise, and ordering tackle components by phone is no exception. You have to put your purchases on a credit card in most instances, and I know that sticks in the craw of a lot of people. If you share this inhibition, it's still worth your while to call up and discuss your problem. You may have to pop for the price of a long-distance call instead of using an 800 number, but you can fill out an order blank while you're on the phone and send it in with a check or money order the first chance you get. My suggestion—an honest one based on a few sad experiences I've had from doing otherwise—is that you establish a long-distance relationship with the catalog people you plan to do business with. I hope you'll listen to your Uncle Jim.

The first thing to do when you begin your adventure into tackle making is to sit down and order a catalog from every house listed in the Appendix of this book that deals in the kind of supplies you'll be needing. Cabela's spring catalog (but, unfortunately, not their others) is a gold mine of tackle components. But you'll have to specify that it's their spring fishing catalog you're interested in.

Bass Pro Shops' annual catalog, which currently sells for two dollars, is a veritable Sears, Roebuck of fishing tackle and components. I frequently thumb through its pages just to get ideas on new lure designs and patterns I want to build. Another thing it does is boost my ego a little when comparing prices for finished lures I know I can make for far less. Their catalog should be part of every fisherman's library.

Two other general-purpose, if somewhat more limited, tackle-component catalog houses are Reed Tackle of Fairfield, New Jersey, and Sportsman's Supply of Toledo, Ohio. Both of them are extremely helpful on the phone and Reed, in particular, has about the fastest response time of any house I've dealt with.

The preeminent supply houses for rod-building supplies have got to be Dale Clemens Custom Tackle of Allentown, Pennsylvania, and Pfeiffer's Tackle Crafters of Phoenix, Maryland. Especially if you live out on the West Coast, you should check out Shoff's Tackle Supplies of Kent, Washington. Delivery time to the Midwest takes about ten days, but they are absolutely the nicest people to deal with that you'll ever find. Other excellent houses specializing in rod-building supplies include Tackle Chandlers of Wilmington, Delaware, and Angler's Workshop of Woodland, Washington. Most of these places also have limited offerings of other tackle-making supplies.

If fly-fishing supplies are what you're after, Ed Hille's outfit, The Angler's Supply House in Williamsport, Pennsylvania, is hard to beat. Hille offers a number of items of his own design, including a line of graphite and fiberglass rod blanks and a really neat kit for tying streamer and bass flies.

If you're into plastic worms—and what bass fisherman isn't?—the place to go for one-piece molds is Lure-Craft Industries of Solsberry, Indiana. Besides offering outstanding molds of every configuration imaginable, this house can provide liquid plastic and virtually every other worm-making supply you ever heard of. Moreover, the price of their unique silicone-rubber molds is surprisingly modest for a unit that will last a lifetime.

I've left one of my favorite catalog houses until last because I think it deserves special mention. That's Netcraft Fishing Tackle of Toledo, Ohio. I'd seen Netcraft's ads in all the outdoor magazines for years, but had never contacted them because I assumed—from their name—that they specialized in nets and seines. That's the way they got started back in 1941, but today they offer one of the most comprehensive lines of tackle-making components to be found anywhere. I've now corrected my oversight, and have found them to be delightful people to deal with in every respect. (They even included a refund check with my last order because I'd overpaid.) Don't make the same mistake I did; contact them for sure.

I'm sure that there must be some unpleasant people working for catalog houses, and they undoubtedly have bad days just like all the rest of us. I'm equally sure that every now and then they'll screw up one of your orders, just as they have mine. On balance, though, my dealings with them have been honest, straightforward, and altogether pleasant. I'm confident that yours will be, too. And for a guy whose wife can't get him to go shopping, that's quite an admission.

5. Building Your Own Rods

It used to be that fishing-rod construction was kind of like the Volkswagen Beetle—nothing ever changed. Well, for sure, it ain't that way no more. Nowadays, you can't pick up an outdoors magazine without discovering that some manufacturer has gone and invented a better way of making rods.

Moreover, I'm obliged to say that most of the developments aren't just advertising hype: they really do represent advancements that make fishing more pleasurable. Better yet, the number of rod-building components available to home craftsmen is greater—if somewhat more confusing—than ever before.

Undeniably the single most important component of rod construction is the rod blank, or shaft. A decade or so ago, nearly all finished rods and blanks were made of hollow glass. Fiberglass construction, in fact, revolutionized rod building during those invention-filled years following World War II. By the time hollow glass came along, good-quality rods made of split bamboo were already priced out of reach for many fishermen, and metals such as steel, alloyed aluminum, and beryllium copper had taken over much of the market.

After a period of trial and error, glass proved itself superior to all of them: it was cheaper, stronger, lighter, and more sensitive then anything made before, and American fishermen welcomed it with open arms. Periodic improvements over the years—both in the fiberglass itself and in the bonding resins that held it together—had most of us convinced that the golden age of rod building was at hand.

Then, about a dozen years ago, we began hearing about a new space-age material called graphite. Ounce for ounce, it offered even better sensitivity and strength than hollow glass, and its superior ability to store and release energy made it easier for the average fisherman to make longer and more accurate casts. Just about the time many of us were replacing our old fiberglass rods with ones made of graphite, still another wonder material—something called boron—made its debut.

Now, I strongly suspect that it was at about this point that just a touch of Madison Avenue may have entered the picture. Whereas graphite is measurably and demonstrably superior to fiberglass in a number of important characteristics, the margin that boron enjoys over graphite is significantly less. Moreover, boron fibers cost the manufac-

The Rod Blank

25

A Comparison of Fibers

turer about five times as much as graphite—a factor that's reflected in the price of boron blanks and finished rods.

I think it might be worth our while at this point to take a look at just what the three most important materials used in rod construction really are.

Fiberglass is made by flowing molten glass through tiny orifices in a melting furnace. The glass strands are pulled through the little holes at high speed and stretched, while partially molten, into fine fibers or filaments. These fibers are then processed and woven into yarns or fabrics. Of the types of glass available, E-glass has been the most widely used for rod construction because of its good water resistance and high tensile modulus (ability to resist deformation and give a good stiffness-to-weight ratio). A newer type of glass, called S-glass, has an even higher tensile modulus (by about 30 percent) and is about midway between E-glass and graphite in price and performance.

Graphite is produced by passing a polymer fiber (which looks a lot like superfine monofilament fishing line) through a heated vacuum until only carbon atoms remain in the finished fiber. The resulting tensile modulus is four to eight times that of fiberglass, which allows a graphite rod to have thinner walls and a more slender configuration than its fiberglass counterpart. This accounts for the greater strength and lightness of graphite rods.

But graphite (and boron, too) has something else going for it. A combination of fiber configuration and bonding properties enhances unidirectional fiber alignment. This, in turn, means that graphite and boron rods can be designed with unbroken fibers extending all the way from butt to tip. This construction provides smoother energy release and gives better casting quality as well as greatly improved sensitivity.

So what about boron? Well, I think the jury is still out on whether this material is going to make a really important contribution to rod making. Boron fiber is produced by the reduction of boron-containing gas in contact with a heated filament, usually a tungsten alloy. While the tensile strength of the resulting fiber is greater than graphite, the filament itself is heavier and contributes to the overall weight of the fiber. Because of this, boron fibers have been used so far in combination with much larger amounts of graphite fibers. I don't know of a single manufacturer that is using much more than about 15 percent boron in its rods, and some use even less.

The technology involved in designing graphite and graphite-boron rods is extremely complex. Not only must those tiny fibers be arranged uniformly around the forming mandrel (as with fiberglass), they must also be unidirectionally aligned butt to tip. The manufacturers that have succeeded in doing this are producing the finest rod blanks ever made. Those that aren't are producing junk—regardless of how much graphite or boron content they claim for their product.

The inclusion of boron fibers in a rod, if done correctly, improves its sensitivity by maybe 20 to 30 percent over that of a corresponding graphite rod, but that's nowhere near the improvement that graphite provides over fiberglass. The other thing I wonder is simply this: Are my tired old reflexes up to the challenge of setting that hook in the few milliseconds provided by the additional sensitivity of boron?

George Loechi, editor of *Fishing Tackle Trade News*, makes this interesting analogy: "If the human ear is unable to hear the high-pitched sound of a dog whistle, why build a hi-fi set that's capable of reproducing it?" Loechi and other experts I've talked with think the addition of boron fibers to rod blanks may be one more bell or whistle than most fishermen are prepared to cope with.

Taper, Action, and Power

I suspect there's been more confusion about taper, action, and power—and the relative terms used to describe them—than any other aspect of rod building. The manufacturers and sellers themselves haven't helped a whole lot, describing as they do the characteristics of their respective products in terms that are both contradictory and confusing. Let me make a stab at clearing away some of the cobwebs.

Taper is an expression of how rapidly the diameter of a rod shaft graduates from tip to butt. If the taper is gradual, the rod is spoken of as having a "slow" or "progressive" taper. A "fast" taper, on the other hand, indicates that the rod's tip is of a much smaller diameter than its butt. Taper influences both the action and power of a rod, more so in fiberglass construction than in graphite and graphite-boron construction with their unidirectional fiber alignment.

Rod action, no matter how often it's used incorrectly, describes the point at which a rod bends or "unloads" its energy when casting or fighting a fish. A rod with a "fast" or "tippy" action has a flexible tip and a relatively stiff butt. What's known as "slow" or "parabolic" action is just the reverse—when a rod with this action is flexed, its bend extends throughout the entire length of the shaft. Here's the way Fenwick and a few other manufacturers define the relationship between rod curvature and the terms used to describe action:

Point of Curvature	*Descriptive Term*
Upper ¼ of shaft	Extra fast
Upper ⅓ of shaft	Fast
Upper ½ of shaft	Moderate
Tip to butt	Slow

The dictionary defines power as the possession of control or authority. As applied to rods, power describes the size of the line and lures (and, of course, the fish) that the rod is designed to handle. Power is a function of the diameter of the rod's butt in relation to its length. To describe this aspect of a rod's performance, most tackle makers use such terms as "light," "medium," "heavy," and a whole bunch of intermediate terms their copywriters have dreamed up. A rod designated as an "ultralight," for example, is typically expected to handle two- to six-pound test line and lures in the range of ⅟₃₂ to ⅛ ounce. It would be fine for crappie and other panfish, but you wouldn't want to fight a big northern or largemouth with it. No two rod makers designate power alike, and there's considerable overlap between designations. The following table, for which I bear sole responsibility, will give you a rough idea of how power relates to line test and lure weights.

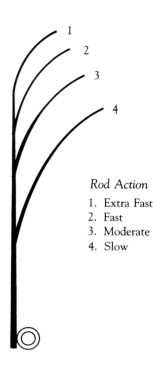

Rod Action
1. Extra Fast
2. Fast
3. Moderate
4. Slow

Power Designation	Line Size (lbs.)	Lure Weight (oz.)
Ultralight Spinning	2–6	1/32–1/8
Light Spinning	4–8	1/16–3/8
Medium Spinning	6–12	1/4–5/8
Heavy Spinning	8–17	3/8–1 1/4
Light Casting	8–12	1/4–5/8
Medium Light Casting	10–15	3/8–3/4
Medium Casting	12–17	1/2–1
Medium Heavy Casting	15–20	3/4–1 1/2
Heavy Casting	17–30	1 1/4–2

I frankly doubt there will ever be a uniform system of designating the power and action of rods; there are just too many types of rods being made and too many people making them. Nor am I sure that a uniform system, were it possible to devise one, would be all that helpful to all that many fishermen. I say this because I believe that the action and power of rods are hands-on, subjective determinations best made by individual preferences and angling requirements.

Selecting the Right Blank

It's axiomatic to observe that the best way to determine whether the power and action of a rod fit your needs is to fish with it. It's no less self-evident that such is seldom possible prior to the purchase of a finished rod, and quite impossible when ordering rod blanks from a catalog house. For better or worse, the home craftsman is locked into understanding and trusting the action and power designations provided by rod manufacturers and then discussing his needs with the customer service reps at one or more catalog houses. Here are a few general observations, based on the primary duties a rod is expected to perform, that I think may help you.

CASTING

The best action for long, precision casting is a slow or parabolic one that allows the rod to store and unload its energy all the way from tip to butt. This sort of action is best illustrated by fly-rod design, which helps the angler transfer all the energy in his cast to the line and leader. A similar situation applies in casting extremely light (1/32- to 1/16-ounce) lures with spinning gear. Here's where a lot of novice fishermen go astray, because they confuse ultralight power with fast action. 'Tain't that way at all. If long casts with light tackle is your objective, select the slowest action you can find. Also, other things being equal, a long rod will cast farther than a shorter one of comparable power and action, because tip velocity is directly proportional to rod length.

SENSITIVITY

This highly desirable rod characteristic for many fishing situations is what enables the angler to "feel" light strikes or "bumps." It's not as directly related to a rod's action and power as it is to the rod's construction and composition. Here, more than anywhere else, is where graphite and boron have the edge. Also, of course, the rod shaft doesn't act alone, but in concert with line, reel, reel seat, and handle. Generally speaking, a slow tip-to-butt action has a slight edge over faster actions for transmitting energy, but so many other factors come into play that nothing more than generalization is possible. A well-balanced unit is perhaps your most important attribute.

28

The ideal rod construction for hook setting calls for considerable stiffness throughout most of the rod's length, so that minimal delay occurs between the strike and the angler's reaction to it. Also, stiffness maximizes the amount of line taken up and compensates for line stretch and slack. The bass fisherman's worm rod, with its heavy power and fast action, is perhaps the best example of this type of construction. Unfortunately, the best design for hook setting isn't best for casting and sensitivity, so some compromise is often desirable. My personal preference in a worm rod is moderate to fast action and medium power.

The best rod design for fighting and landing fish is one in which the butt section is substantially bigger than the tip. Rods of this design, often called "magnum action" or "fast taper," are popular for offshore fishing and for trout and salmon trolling on the Great Lakes. Most of the action in this type of rod occurs in the upper third of the shaft, while the butt section is stiff and inflexible. While such rods won't "bottom out"— that is, exceed their limits of elasticity—they're poor casting tools because of their inability to store and release energy.

It's obvious from the foregoing that nearly all rod construction involves some compromises. Some of the qualities we seek complement one another, but a lot of them work in opposite directions. The blank to buy is the one that offers the largest number of characteristics you want in the rod you build.

Choosing the rod blank for the kind of fishing you have in mind is the most important selection you have to make when you set about building your own rod. Picking the proper parts to balance and complement the blank of your choosing is a no less important, if somewhat less demanding, decision.

Selecting Other Rod Components

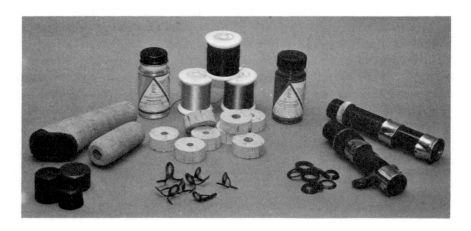

Depending on the construction method selected, the essentials of rod building may include a formed handle consisting of butt grips and foregrips, guides and tiptop, color preserver and varnish, winding thread, cork rings (for handle and/or reel-seat bushing), winding checks or hosels, and reel seats.

One way to go—and I recommend it for first-time rod builders—is to settle on one of the rod-building kits offered by several of the catalog houses. They differ from ordering individual components only to the extent that everything necessary to building a finished rod (with the exception of varnish and winding thread) has been selected for you. If you find what you have in mind among the twenty or so kits usually offered, it assures that your first order will include everything you need.

Depending upon the type of rod you want to build and the method of construction you decide on, you'll require such ancillary parts as handle, reel seat, guides and tiptop, butt cap, winding check, thread, and, if you want to use it, butt-wind tape. Additionally, as a coating for the thread you will use to fix the guides to the shaft, you will need a good rod varnish and color preserver. The use of these components will be discussed in detail as we go through the steps of rod building, but first let's take a brief look at the function served by each part and the materials from which they are typically made.

HANDLES

The function of the rod handle requires no great elaboration. For many years, cork was the most comfortable and efficient material available for quality handle construction. It remains an excellent choice, but in recent years soft (resilient) plastic—notably vinyl and hypalon—have begun to replace cork on quality rods. Until recently, the shafts of most casting rods were affixed to the handles by simply gluing them in place or by fitting them with butt ferrules that went into chucks like those on hand drills. A newer and much improved method of construction calls for the blank to be extended all the way through the handles in what is known as "through-the-handle" or unitary construction. Unitary construction greatly improves the sensitivity of a rod by making the shaft and handle perform as a single unit. Both Fenwick and Fuji make excellent unitary handles.

REEL SEATS

Designed for no purpose other than to hold the reel in place on the rod, reel seats have been made in a number of ways and of many materials. Metal, most often an aluminum alloy, was the material of choice for many years, but lately it has been replaced in some applications (notably spinning and casting rods) by fiberglass and graphite. The reel seat and handle are constructed as a single unit in some of the newer offerings, particularly those intended for through-the-handle construction. Various methods are used to secure the reel foot to the seat, with the "skip-and-screw" technique predominating in casting rods, and threaded retaining rings used most often on spinning and fly rods. The simplest (and some feel the best) method of securing spinning reels consists of two nonthreaded retaining rings that slide over the reel foot to mount it directly on the handle. No reel seat, as such, is used in this method— the advantage of which is that it allows the reel to be placed anywhere along the handle.

Some fishermen prefer nonthreaded retaining rings instead of a reel seat for attaching their spinning reels to the handle of a rod.

Many, but not all, reel seats require that a bushing or adapter be placed between the reel seat and the rod blank. Usually made of cork or tape, the bushing serves to cushion the blank and fill the space between it and the reel seat. Bushings are available in several inside and outside diameters to fit most blanks and seats, but sizing with a rasp and/or sandpaper is usually required. Masking tape wrapped at spaced intervals around the blank works as well as anything I've used, and is easy to apply.

REEL-SEAT BUSHINGS

The function of guides, as the name implies, is to guide the line smoothly and effortlessly along the rod shaft. A tiptop is simply the guide that is fitted on the tip of the rod and glued in place. Most guides are measured, in millimeters, by *outside* diameter, but a few manufacturers continue to state the *inside* diameter of their guides. Be sure, when you order, which you are getting. Tiptops are measured in sixty-fourths of an inch (i.e., a size 5.0 tiptop has an inside diameter of 5/64 inch). Gauges designed to measure tiptops are available.

GUIDES AND TIPTOPS

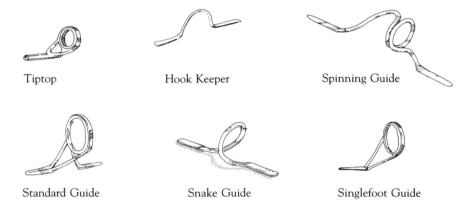

Rod Guides

Tiptop   Hook Keeper   Spinning Guide

Standard Guide   Snake Guide   Singlefoot Guide

Once restricted to metal, guides and tiptops are now being made from such exotic materials as ceramic, silicon carbide, and aluminum oxide. My choice, from the standpoint of cost and serviceability, is aluminum oxide. Guides should be just as light as possible for the purpose intended, and the feet should be flexible so as not to interfere with rod action. Single-foot guides, although slightly more difficult to wrap, are a good choice for light rods. The size and number of guides, and their placement on the blank (as will be discussed shortly), is critical to good rod performance.

Nylon is today's near-universal choice for thread used to wrap guides. It comes in numerous sizes and colors to complement the power and color of your rod blank. Thread used for rod-making chores is sized A, D, E, EE, and FF, with A being the lightest and FF the heaviest. As a practical matter, though, sizes A and D are all that many rod builders ever use—A for ultralight spinning and fly rods, and D for everything else. Size E is useful for the heaviest freshwater casting rods; size EE is best for surf, boat, and trolling rods, and FF for the heaviest offshore rods.

WINDING THREAD

31

I've found size-D thread well suited to 90 percent of my rod-building efforts. A fifty-yard spool—the smallest available—will wrap several rods, but I prefer to buy mine in hundred-yard spools simply because they're easier to keep up with. A typical (not fancy) rod requires two colors of thread: one for the master wrap and the other for the trim wrap. If you put a diamond wrap on the butt section, you'll want at least a third (and possibly a fourth) color.

VARNISH AND COLOR PRESERVER

Back in the days of split bamboo, rod varnish was used to coat the entire rod. No rod blank being made today benefits from varnishing, and doing so can adversely affect its performance. Nowadays, varnish is used only to coat winding thread once the wrappings are in place, both to protect the thread and to cement it to the blank. Several good varnishes are available, but the best of them are those with a liquid plastic (polyurethane) base. I've never had it crack or yellow on me, which is more than I can say for the older types.

Color preserver serves only to keep the varnish from discoloring the thread. Most rod builders put three or four coats of color preserver (the stuff dries immediately) under an equal number of coats of varnish. Gudebrod makes a colorfast thread called NCP (for "no color preservative") that eliminates the need for using preserver. Two-part (epoxy) finishes are also finding some acceptance among rod builders, but it's a lot of trouble to mix and use, and I don't personally care for the slick look it gives.

BUTT CAPS

These little gizmos are fitted over the handles of all rods except those having pistol-type grips. Their purpose is to protect the handle and to give it a finished look. Most of the butt caps used today are plastic jobs that resemble chair or crutch tips, but wood and machined-metal ones of German silver and aluminum are also available if you really want to dress up your rod. A butt cap should be purchased with an inside diameter slightly smaller than the outside diameter of the butt grip, and the latter rasped down to fit before gluing the cap in place.

WINDING CHECKS AND HOSELS

Really nothing more than rubber or plastic washers, winding checks and hosels are fitted on the rod blank immediately forward of the handle to give a finished appearance to the foregrip. Winding checks are typically slightly dished, round discs with holes in the middle. Hosels serve the same purpose as winding checks, but come in different shapes. Hosels are usually used on larger rods, but an extremely attractive appearance can be achieved on casting rods by using butt caps and hosels of matching wood. Winding checks and hosels are glued in place as the final step of handle construction *before* the wrapping operation gets underway.

FERRULES

Nowhere has rod-making technology advanced more than in the elimination of the metal ferrules once used to join together rod sections in two-piece and multiple-piece (backpack rod) construction. In place of the old metal units, which dampened rod action and destroyed the appearance of an otherwise uncluttered rod shaft, virtually all makers of quality rod blanks have gone to glass-to-glass or graphite-to-graphite ferrules.

Three basic methods are used in this type of construction. In the first, a solid or heavy-walled plug or dowel of the same composition as the blank is inserted in the larger (butt) section of the blank, and the hollow end of the tip section is fitted over the protruding end of the dowel. In the second method, a hollow sleeve—again of the same composition as the blank—is epoxied into place on the tip section of the rod and the butt section slipped into the open sleeve to form a union. In yet a third approach, what amounts to two separate rod blanks are made, and the hollow end of one is slipped over the smaller end of the other.

Each of these methods provides a two-piece shaft with structual integrity rivaling that of single-piece construction. All major manufacturers now offer factory-ferruled blanks that employ one of these three methods. I do advise that you put windings around both the male and female sections of the ferrule at the time you wrap your guides. Aside from repairing broken shafts, there's little reason for the home craftsman ever to be bothered with ferrule installation.

ADHESIVES

Any number of different glues, cements, and two-part epoxies are used in rod building, and several special-purpose adhesives are available from the catalog houses. Actually, however, only two or three basic types are required, and all are readily available through hardware and home-repair stores.

You will use adhesives for three basic purposes in building a rod: for cementing the handle to the blank; for cementing the reel seat to the blank; and for gluing the tiptop to the end of the rod. Some builders prefer to use slow-cure, flexible epoxies for cementing their handles. This is what I use for preformed pistol-grip construction, but for cork-ring grips I prefer a contact cement such as Duro or Pliobond. These cements clean up easily with lacquer thinner and will enable you to replace broken or worn sections of the grip more readily. A somewhat more viscous glue is preferable for cementing the reel seat and its bushing, and for this purpose I use a *filled* epoxy such as that available from Weldwood. Tiptops, which often require replacement, shouldn't be permanently mounted at all. For this purpose, a hot-melt glue is the only way to go. Small sticks of this type of glue are available at most tackle shops, and many fishermen carry a stick in their tackle boxes.

Making Your Rod-Wrapping Jig

Rod-wrapping jigs (or racks) serve no purpose other than to hold the blank firmly and enable you to turn it as you wrap on winding thread to hold the guides in place and decorate the blank. You can, if you want, spend up to $150 for an elaborate wrapping jig, or you can go to the other extreme and make one that's reasonably serviceable out of two bent coathangers.

Spending big bucks for a wrapping jig makes no sense at all to me, and I find coathangers a tad too springy for my taste. So I go an intermediate route and make a rod-wrapping jig from 1-by-4-inch pine boards and four fairly large (2-inch) casters such as those used on TV trays.

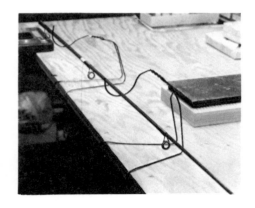

The simplest rod-wrapping jig is made by bending two coat hangers. The author, however, feels that jigs made this way are too springy and fail to give good control during the wrapping process.

The pine boards are cut to 4- and 10-inch lengths (two of each) and fixed together to form two L-shaped supports. Two holes are then bored into the upper ends of the longer (upright) legs of the L's to hold the casters. Drill the holes close enough together so that the casters have just enough room between them to rotate freely.

In use, the L-shaped supports, or stanchions, are secured to the top of your workbench with C-clamps at a convenient distance apart for the work you are doing (usually 18 to 24 inches).

The upright legs of the stanchions can be more or less than 10 inches in height, depending on the height of your workbench and on whether you prefer to work standing or sitting. The top of my bench is 41 inches from the floor, and I prefer to do my rod wrapping while standing, so a 10-inch length puts the rod blank at a comfortable height for me. Some of the commercially made wrapping jigs have uprights that are only 5 or 6 inches high, so my choice is far from universal.

Most of the commercial jigs hold the rod blank in simple V- or U-shaped slots cut into their uprights. The slots are then lined with felt or other soft material so the blank doesn't become scarred or defaced. There's nothing wrong with this approach; I simply find that using casters allows the blank to turn more freely.

Winding thread must be under tension as you wrap it onto the blank. For about six dollars you can buy thread-tension hardware consisting of two cupped discs held together on a stud with a beehive spring. They work well. But an equally good approach that costs nothing consists of putting the thread spool in a cup or large-mouth jar (such as a peanut butter jar) and applying tension by running the thread through the pages of an old book weighted with a piece of plate iron or a couple more books. Do be sure it's an *old* book, as the thread will cut into its pages. In use, the book is simply placed on your workbench a foot or so behind the stanchions (held by C-clamps on the front of the workbench), and the thread-holding jar a few inches behind the book. Assuming your workbench top is at least twenty inches deep, you'll have plenty of room.

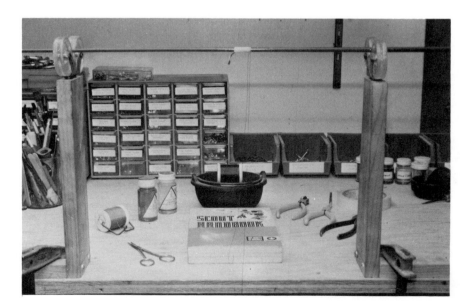

The author's choice in a rod-wrapping jig, construction of which is described in the text, consists of two L-shaped stanchions topped by large plastic casters. Note that winding thread is passed through book for tension.

All rods, especially those in which fiberglass accounts for all or part of their composition (and this includes many graphite blanks), have a spine—a slightly more powerful side. This results from the way in which the glass cloth is wound onto the mandrel as rods are constructed. For precision casting, this spine must be aligned with the guides, which means you need to locate the stiff side of the rod blank. On spinning and fly rods, the guides should be mounted *opposite* the spine, so they will be facing the water as you cast. On casting rods, the guides should be mounted *along* the spine, so that they face over your shoulder as you cast. If the guides are not aligned on or opposite the spine—that is, if the spine is off to one side of the guides—you'll find that your rod has a tendency to cast to one side or the other. If you've ever used a cheaply built rod that had this tendency, you know how aggravating it can be to have to compensate for your casts every time.

To locate the spine of a newly received blank, rest its butt on a smooth, flat surface (such as a concrete floor) and angle the blank at about 45 degrees. Support the rod near its tip with the palm of one hand and press down on the blank near its middle with the fingers of your other hand. Now, slowly roll the blank back and forth, while bent, until you locate the point at which it seems to jump a little. This point is the location of the spine. If you are working with a two-piece rod, the tip and butt sections should be joined together while locating the spine. Join the sections so that the completed blank is as straight as possible, but don't worry about a slight curvature, as most rods have one.

Because of the difference in the way they are constructed (unidirectional fiber alignment), rods with a high percentage of graphite and graphite-boron have little spine. (Even some ultralight fiberglass rods have spines that aren't all that pronounced.) If you're unable to locate the spine of the blank you're using, don't let it concern you too much. If no spine is discernible, sight along the blank by holding the butt to your eye and determine any slight curvature it may have. Then mount the guides along the *outside* of the curve.

Having found the spine (or, alternatively, the curvature) of the blank, use a permanent felt-tip pen to mark—at three or four places—the side on which you will mount the guides. A permanent marker won't rub off as you handle the blank, but is easily removed with rubbing alcohol (or Jack Daniel's, if you prefer) once the guides are wrapped.

No matter what kind of rod you're building, construction *always* proceeds from butt to tip. This means the handle assembly, including the reel seat, is your first order of business. In some types of construction, the entire handle assembly comes as a single unit. In such instances, the assembly is simply fitted over the butt and cemented in place (following placement and gluing of an adapter, if one is required). The winding check is then slipped over the rod tip and glued in place snug against the foregrip.

In other types of construction (where butt grip, reel seat, and foregrip come as separate pieces), the handle component *closest to the butt* is the first to be sized and glued in place. In assembling a fly rod, for example, the sequence will be (1) reel seat, (2) grip, and (3) winding check. For casting and spinning rods, the sequence is (1) butt grip, (2) butt cap,

Aligning the Blank

The spine of a rod is located by flexing the blank and slowly rolling it between one's hands.

Assembling the Handle

35

(3) reel-seat bushing, (4) reel seat, (5) foregrip, and (6) winding check.

As you begin gluing your handle assembly in place, be *sure* that the grips and reel-seat hood are in perfect alignment with the marks you have made to show where the guides will be placed.

USING CORK RINGS

If you elect to build your handle from cork rings rather than preformed grips, use a rat-tail rasp to enlarge the inside diameters of each ring, remembering that those closest to the butt will have slightly larger holes than those closer to the tip. Fit the cork rings into place by sliding them down over the tip to the butt. Close tolerances are preferred, but not so tight as to risk splitting the cork rings.

With the cork rings in position and proper sequence (it doesn't hurt to number them as you enlarge their holes), cement them to the blank and to each other, beginning at the butt and progressing toward the tip. As noted earlier, I prefer a good-quality contact (rubber base) cement for the purpose, but a flexible (slow-cure) epoxy gives more permanent bonding.

MAKING A GLUING JIG

To hold the cork rings in mild compression while the cement cures, make a simple vise from 1-by-2-inch scrap lumber and dowel rods. Begin by cutting two 8- to 10-inch lengths from the one-by-two and drilling holes the same diameter as your dowel about 1½ inches from the end of each piece. The holes will go all the way through one piece and halfway through the other. Clamp the pieces together as you drill the holes so that the holes are perfectly aligned. Now, in the center of the one-by-two that you've drilled holes all the way through, drill another hole that's slightly larger than the butt section of your rod blank.

A simple but effective jig for holding cork rings in compression during gluing can be made from scrap lumber, dowels, and rubber bands cut from an inner tube.

Cut a dowel in half so that each resulting piece is about 18 inches long. Glue one end of each dowel into the blind holes you've drilled in one of your one-by-twos, and slide the other one-by-two down over the dowels about halfway to hold them in position until the glue dries. In use, the one-by-two with the dowels glued in it is placed over the butt of the rod, and the one-by-two with a hole in its center is passed down the rod blank and onto the other (open) end of the dowels, sandwiching your glued cork rings between the boards. Place large rubber bands or adjustable clamps over both ends of the boards to hold the rings in compression until the glue has cured.

With your butt grip securely glued, remove the gluing jig and use a half-moon rasp or heavy sandpaper to rough-finish the grip to approximately the size and configuration you want to end up with. Now, before going any further, mark the point at which the butt cap will fit down over the grip. Wrap several thicknesses of masking tape over the handle at this point and, using the tape as a guide, reduce the circumference of the grip behind the tape so that the butt cap fits snugly over it. Remove the tape from the grip and wrap another piece of tape around the butt-cap cutout you've just made. Build up the tape until the wrap equals the outside diameter of the cap. This tape will be your guide as you finish the remainder of the butt grip with progressively finer grades of sandpaper.

Completing Your Handle

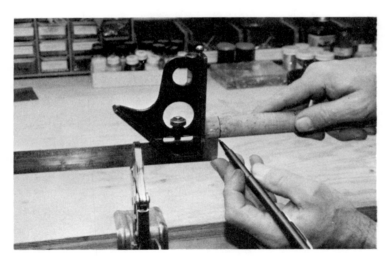

In straight-handle construction, location of butt cap should be marked after handle has been roughed out.

Rasp and sand end of handle to make it fit the inside diameter of the butt cap.

37

*Use contact cement to glue
the butt cap in place.*

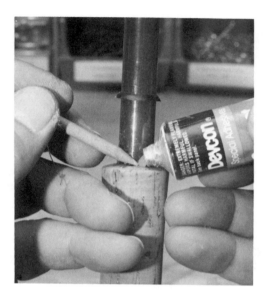

*Handle construction is completed
by gluing the winding check on
blank ahead of foregrip.*

The best thing about cork-ring construction is that you can make a
grip that fits your hand exactly, no matter how big or small it may be.
The only thing you have to keep in mind is that the forward (toward
the rod tip) end of the butt grip and the rear end of the foregrip must
match up with the circumference of the reel seat you are using. Most
builders like to wait until they have the entire handle assembly glued
into place before putting the final sanding touches on their grips. If you
go this route, be sure to mask off the reel seat and a few inches of the
rod blank ahead of the foregrip so you don't scratch them while sanding.

INSTALLING THE REEL SEAT   With the butt grip glued and roughed out, you're ready to install the
reel seat. First, slide the seat down the blank and determine how much
space exists between it and the blank. This space must be filled with
cork, fiber (wrapped cord), or masking tape. Some builders swear, and
I tend to agree, that nothing cushions the blank as well as cork. If you
want to use this method of making a reel-seat bushing, repeat the procedure you used to make your butt grip, rasping down the outside diameter of the rings until the reel seat slides over them. Again, use contact cement or a slow-cure epoxy to glue the rings to each other and to
the blank.

A much simpler technique for making the reel-seat bushing—and one I believe adequate for all except the heaviest-duty rods—calls for wrapping three to five strips of masking tape around the blank until the proper buildup is achieved. Assuming a typical reel-seat length of 5 inches, four wraps of ¾-inch masking tape works out about right. The important thing is to leave a little space between the tape wraps. Because of its ease and simplicity, this is the method I usually use.

Simplest method of reel-seat bushing construction calls for several parallel wraps of masking tape, coated with filled epoxy to bond reel seat to both bushing and blank.

A third method of reel-seat bushing construction involves a continuous wrap of fibrous cord around the blank. It's not as good as cork and not as easy as masking tape, so I seldom use it. But in case anybody ever mentions it, you can say your Uncle Jim told you about it.

Whether you use cork, tape, or cord, the best adhesive for securing the reel seat to its bushing is filled epoxy. This material, which has a consistency about like that of pancake batter, fills the voids between the reel seat and the bushing better than anything else. Weldwood makes a resorcinol-based two-part resin that I've found well suited for the purpose.

Mix the epoxy as directed, coat the bushing liberally, and slide the reel seat into place with a rotating motion that distributes the epoxy evenly. If you are using masking tape for the bushing, apply enough epoxy to fill the spaces between the tape wraps as well as coating their surfaces. Be sure to wipe off all extra epoxy before it cures; you'll never get it off afterwards.

At the risk of being redundant, let me remind you again to line up the fixed hood of the reel seat with the marks you've made to indicate guide placement.

Even when I'm using cork rings to make my butt grip, I prefer using preformed cork for the foregrip that's installed after the reel seat is in place. I like this approach because there's no sizing to fit individual hands involved, and it's a lot quicker than cork-ring construction. If a preformed foregrip is used, the only shaping that's usually required is some reaming with a rat-tail rasp to make the grip fit over the blank. Just be sure, when you order, that the supplier sends the size intended for use with the handle assembly you are using.

Every now and then, expecially when retrofitting an old rod, you may find it necessary to build your foregrip from cork rings. When I'm doing

INSTALLING THE FOREGRIP

39

this, I find it best to assemble and glue the rings *before* putting them on the rod blank. I go about this by gluing together enough rings to achieve the grip length I want, then rasping and sanding both their outside and inside dimensions to fit. The reason for doing things this way is simple: Getting the taper you want on a foregrip calls for rasping and sanding down its entire length, and it's the devil's own work to do this without boogering the blank once the grip is glued in place. As previously noted, final sanding is done with the handle assembly completed and masking tape covering vulnerable areas.

When the handle assembly has been given its final sanding, select a winding check of the correct size, slide it over the rod tip, and glue it to the blank and foregrip. I use contact cement to glue the winding check, which is additionally held in place by the butt wrap.

Placing the Guides

Comes now one of the more critical phases of rod building—correctly placing the guides on the blank. To get started, use a hot-melt glue stick to cement the tiptop in position by aligning it with the marks you've made to indicate the spine of the rod. Glue sticks are easy to use. Just hold a match or cigarette lighter to the stick for a moment, then smear the glue on the tip of the rod where the tiptop will fit over it. Now heat the tiptop and slide it into place. Check its alignment by sighting down the blank from butt to tip. Any misplaced glue will peel off with your fingernail after it hardens.

Move Gathering Guide to Obtain Proper Placement

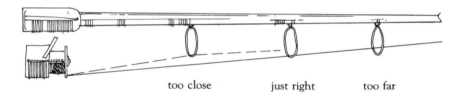

too close just right too far

Place Intermediate Guides (as described in text)

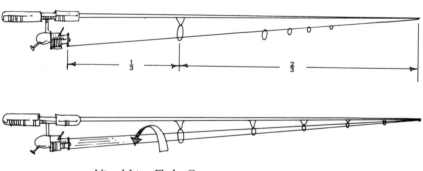

Visual Line Flight Cone

Put the reel you plan to use on its seat and measure the distance between its bail or level-wind to the tiptop. At a point about a third of the way up the blank from the reel, tape the gathering (largest) guide into place. Use masking tape only; anything else is apt to leave a sticky residue that can screw up your windings. Now peel some line off your reel, pass it through the gathering guide, put the remaining guides on the line in proper (largest to smallest) sequence, and tie off the line to the tiptop. Crank up on your reel until the line is tight, but without flexing the rod blank.

Check the position of the butt (gathering) guide. If it constricts the line—that is, puts an angle in it—move it back and forth along the blank until the correct position is obtained. Now position the intermediate guides along the blank so that the outside edges of their rings just touch but don't constrict the line. Tape the guides into place at these points and sight down the back (the side away from the guides) of the rod, tip to butt, to be sure all the guides are lined up along the spine.

With the guides taped in place, flex the rod by tying a weight on the end of the line and letting it hang a few feet below the tip. The line should follow the contour of the rod. If it doesn't, add additional guides, or move the ones already taped in place, until the proper line contour is obtained. There's no precise formula for positioning guides, because all rod blanks are a little different. Trial and error is the only way. But for your effort, you'll get a better-balanced rod than you can buy ready-made (excepting those that are custom-built, of course).

Guide Placement
SPINNING ROD

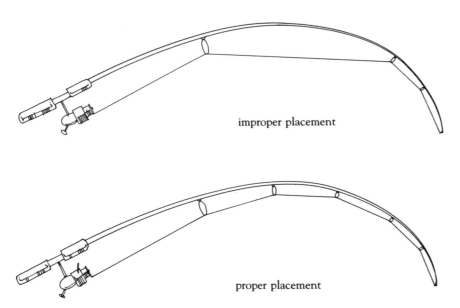

improper placement

proper placement

Now select practice plugs from your tackle box that approximate the lightest and heaviest lures your rod is designed to cast (for example, half to one ounce) and tie them onto your line one at a time. Get out in the backyard or street and lob a few casts. Pay attention to how the rod feels in your hand. Then place a marker at your normal casting distance ahead of you and check the precision of your casts. The crucial questions: Does the line peel off the rod as it should? Are you getting the distance you expect? Are you casting where you aim? Does the rod's action feel good in your hand?

Guide Placement
CASTING ROD

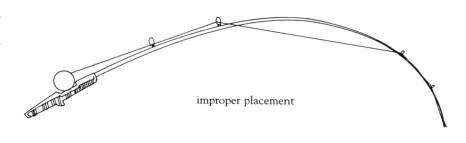

improper placement

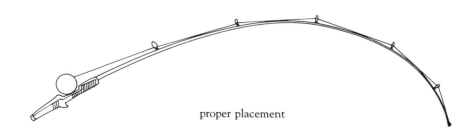

proper placement

Here are some common problems, and their solutions.

1. *Off-center casts*—There's a pretty good chance you've failed to correctly locate the spine. Your handle is already glued in place, of course, but you can improve the situation by moving the guides and tiptop just a few degrees around the blank. I won't say this problem is common, but it does happen every now and then.

2. *Fouled line*—If the line doesn't peel off the reel as it should, your gathering guide is most likely at the wrong distance from the reel. Move it backward or forward just a tad until you find just the right position. Normally, at this point, we're talking fractions of an inch.

3. *Short casts*—If your practice plug isn't getting out there where you think it should, it may be that the line is being constricted by one or more of the intermediate guides. Move the offending guide(s) backward or forward on the blank until the problem is resolved.

4. *Sluggish action*—If your rod shaft doesn't flex where it should like it should, there's a possibility that the guides are too heavy for the blank. This sort of thing occurs most often when you're building an ultralight spinning rod. The action will improve somewhat once the guides are wrapped, but single-foot guides can make a *big* difference.

Wrapping the Guides

Earlier we talked about making a rod-wrapping jig. Now is when you get to use it. Set up your jig as previously described, with the stanchions clamped to your bench top about two feet apart and winding thread passed through the pages of a weighted book. The tension on the thread should grip the guide foot firmly, but allow you to make minor corrections as you wrap.

Only a few supplies are needed for wrapping (winding) rod guides. These include varnish and color preserver, masking tape, hot-melt glue for tiptop, winding thread in two or three colors, plus guides and tiptop.

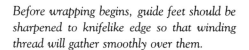

Before wrapping begins, guide feet should be sharpened to knifelike edge so that winding thread will gather smoothly over them.

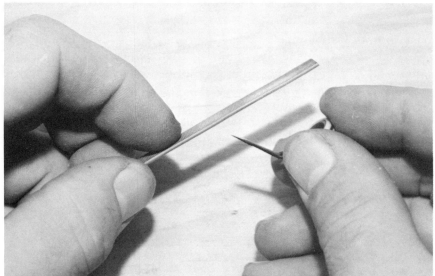

Position the rod blank in the wrapping jig so that the largest (gathering) guide is centered between the stanchions and in line with where the thread comes out of the book. Wrap a piece of masking tape around the shaft to mark where your first wrap will begin. Depending on the size of the guide, the length of the wrap should be anywhere from ½ to 1½ inches. On a typical casting rod, the rear wrap is about 1¼ inches long and the forward wrap about ¾ inch long. It's largely a matter of personal choice, but don't make them any longer than necessary, lest they interfere with the action of your rod.

To begin your wrapping, pull the tag end of the thread back over the rod shaft until you have an excess of maybe three or four inches in hand. Bring the tag end completely around the shaft and lock it into place by forming an X with thread coming off the spool. The wrapping process proceeds by rotating the rod blank *toward* you so you can see the winding thread as it comes onto the blank. Keep your thumb on the tag end until several wraps are made to secure it, then use your thumbnail to scoot the whole works up tight against the masking tape.

X-lock is formed to hold winding thread on the blank.

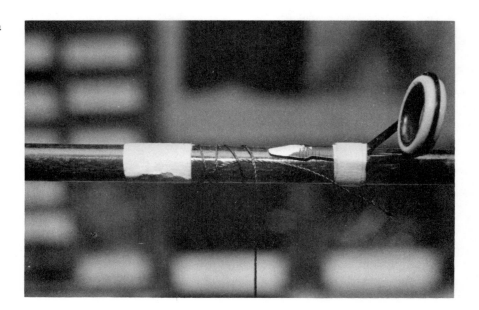

44

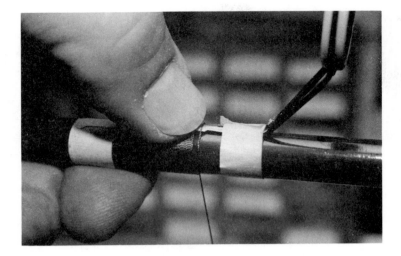

Be sure that thread gathers smoothly over the guide foot.

Keep the line coming onto the shaft at an angle that keeps the wraps tight, but not so acute an angle as to overlap the prior wraps. Just move the blank back and forth in the jig one-half inch or so until you have it right; it only takes a few wraps to get the hang of it. Continue the wrap about halfway up the guide foot, then snip off the tag end with a small scissors or razor blade.

On single-foot guide, masking tape must be cut before winding can proceed.

Now, using a different-color thread, cut off a piece about six inches long and make a loop of it. Lay the looped thread parallel to the shaft and continue your master wrap over it. A pair of pliers draped over the blank at the guide will keep the rod from turning (and thus allowing previously wrapped thread to back off) anytime it's necessary to take your hands off the rod.

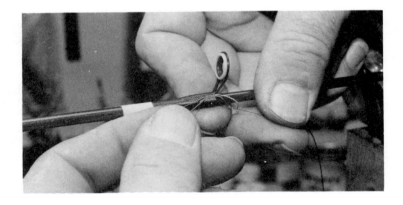

Pull-through loop is tied into master wrap so that tag end can be pulled back through and locked in place.

Continue your wrapping until you reach the point at which the guide foot turns upward into the frame of the guide. Stop your wrapping at this point, as any thread that doesn't lie flat against the blank will break under flex stress when casting. Place your thumb on the end of the thread to hold it tight and cut it midway between the book and the shaft. Now push the cut end through the looped thread and pull it down firmly. Continue holding the cut end firmly between your thumb and forefinger as you pull on the looped thread with the other hand. When the end of the wrapping thread has been pulled under several wraps, release it, but continue pulling on the looped thread until the master thread is all the way through. Trim the excess as close to the wrap as possible with a razor blade or X-acto knife.

Tag end of thread is cut with X-acto knife as close to master wrap as possible to complete winding.

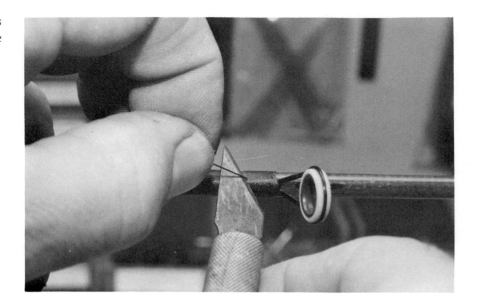

If there's any fuzz on the finished wrap, remove it by singeing lightly with a match or cigarette lighter. (Some builders recommend an alcohol lamp; if you have one, use it.) Now take the handle of the X-acto knife or some other hard, round instrument and burnish the wrap from each end toward the center. Your master wrap is complete.

Though it's only for cosmetic purposes, most rod builders add a trim wrap at the end of their master wrap. I usually do this after all my master wraps (the ones that hold the guides) have been completed. The trim wrap is made with another color thread that complements the master wrap. For example, if the master wrap is done in black or brown, gold or silver gives a pleasing trim wrap.

The trim wrap is done the same way as the master wrap, except the pull-through loop is wrapped under the winding thread immediately. This is necessary because the trim wrap is only about one-quarter inch long, and its entire length is needed to lock the thread in place. Also, the beginning end of the trim wrap is cut off after making only three or four wraps over it. Trim off the finish end of the wrap as closely as possible, then use a round instrument to burnish the wrap and push its loops as close to the master wrap as possible.

46

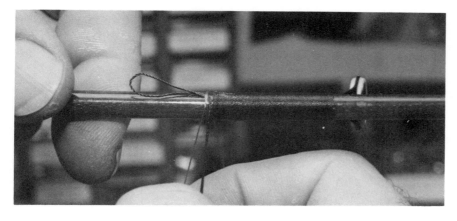

With master wrap complete, trim wrap is added; note that pull-through loop is wrapped in immediately.

Also, for purely cosmetic reasons, I like to wrap the end of the blank for about half an inch below the tiptop. It's not necessary to wrap thread over the shank (barrel) of the tiptop itself.

In two-piece rods, a guide will often be placed just forward of the center ferrule. If possible, position the guide so that its wrapping extends down over the ferrule. In any event, wrap both the male and female portions of the ferrule to impart additional strength. The female portion, in particular, is subject to splitting under heavy fishing pressure unless it is wrapped.

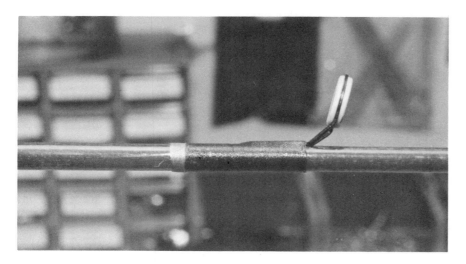

Completed master and trim wrap with one coat of color preserver wiped on. Winding will now proceed up the blank until all guides are wrapped.

Like trim wraps, butt wraps are put on rods for no reason other than to make 'em look "purty." But they've become so much a part of rod-building procedure that a blank without them has an incomplete look about it. Several builders of fine custom rods are known for their highly decorative (and complicated) butt wraps. There are two basic ways of applying butt wraps, so let's discuss the essentials of both.

This is how the butts of all fine rods were once finished, but nowadays you'll find it on only those that are custom built. It's a little tricky, but with a trial run or two, you'll have it mastered.

Applying Butt Wraps

THE DIAMOND WRAP

47

Begin with an underwrap that's necessary to hold the diamond pattern in place. It's done exactly the same way you did your guide wraps. The underwrap can be any length you want, but 3 or 4 inches is usual. My preference is to make the underwrap 3½ inches long, then add a half-inch trim wrap. Start the underwrap at the butt end of the blank, right up next to the winding check. Lock it in with an X-wind just as you did the guide wraps. Any color thread can be used, but I usually opt for the same color used for the master (guide) wraps. The important thing is that the color contrast with those selected for the diamond pattern that follows.

To begin butt wrap, wind on underwrap that extends about 4 inches up blank from fore-grip.

With the underwrap completed, use a felt-tip pen to mark with tiny dots the points along the top and bottom (as lined up with the guides) of the blank where you want the diamonds to intersect. Dots placed one-half inch apart will result in diamonds with center lines spaced an inch apart. As you become more proficient, you may want to make smaller diamonds, but I recommend this size for your initial efforts.

For the diamond pattern, select threads in two or three colors that complement one another. For my center thread—the one that's wrapped on first—I like to use the same color used for my trim wraps.

Begin your diamond wrap by taping (with quarter-inch masking tape) the center thread to the blank at the butt. Wrap the tape around the blank three or four times, because it serves to protect the underwrap when thread used for the diamond wrap is cut. Keeping tension on your center thread by passing it through the weighted book, guide the first spiral so that it passes over every other dot you've made on the underwrap along the top and bottom of the blank. (Some builders prefer to remove the blank from the wrapping jig and to point first the tip and then the butt away from them at a 45-degree angle. I've personally found this approach more difficult, but you can try it and see how it works for you.)

As you rotate the blank to wrap on the spirals, remember that subsequent spirals will make the diamond patterns much thicker than when you begin. For this reason, it's important that the center thread stop short of the end of the underwrap, so that subsequent spirals don't go off its end. I've found that half an inch is a safe distance for a two- or three-thread diamond wrap, but wider patterns (more thread) require additional space.

Center thread is spiraled over the underwrap, up the blank, and back down to the foregrip.

When your beginning spiral wrap is completed, the thread will be back at the handle. Make three or four wraps around the tape to secure it, then wrap back up the left (or right, if you prefer) side of the original wrap. You're going to find that keeping the thread snugged up against the preceding wrap is more difficult over an underwrap, so use your thumbnail as you go along to maintain tight wraps. When your second wrap is back at the handle, again secure the thread with a few quick wraps around the tape, and make another spiral down the right (or opposing) side of the center thread. Repeat this procedure until the center wrap consists of four to six strands of thread. Remember to make successive wraps first on one side, then the other, of the center thread. If you're doing it right, tiny, interlocking diamond patterns will begin to emerge where the thread intersects.

Make a few more wraps around the tape and tie the center wrap off with two or three half-hitches. Cut off the center thread and pass your second thread through the book. Wrap the second thread around the tape a few times to secure it. Now proceed just as you did with the center thread, making spirals first on one side and then the other of the pattern you've laid down. Depending on how wide you want your diamonds, make three to six spirals with the second-color thread. If I plan to use a third-color thread, I wrap on three spirals of my second color; if not, I use four to six spirals to approximate the width of my center wrap. Tie off the second thread just as you did the first.

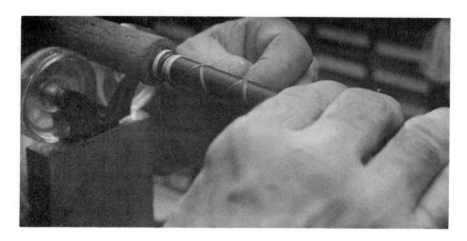

After about five spirals of the center thread are wrapped on, a second color of thread is added. Note that winding thread is tied off over masking tape at winding check.

If you're using a third-color thread, proceed just as you did for the first and second colors, but this time make only two wraps on each side of the pattern already laid down. You can wrap on as many as four or five different colors of thread, if you wish. For an attractive pattern, each successive color band should be slightly narrower (by at least two strands of thread) than the one preceding it.

Two-thread diamond wrap has been completed. A third color of thread can be added if desired.

Now to lock it all together. Beginning at the center of the diamond closest to the handle, overwrap the diamond pattern with the same color thread you used for the center spiral. Bring the overwrap to within a fraction of an inch of the masking tape and, using draped pliers to keep the rod from turning in the wrapping jig, use an X-acto knife or razor blade to cut the threads you've wrapped around the tape. Be careful not to cut through the tape and into the underwrap. With small (fly-tying) scissors, snip off all the tag ends of thread a fraction of an inch ahead of the overwrap. Peel off the masking tape and complete the overwrap right up to the winding check. Don't forget to wrap in a pull-through loop so you can lock the overwrap in place.

Overwrap is added, beginning at center of diamond closest to winding check (foregrip).

As a final step, wind on a trim wrap the same color as your locking overwrap just ahead of the underwrap you laid down before beginning the diamond pattern. Both the overwrap and trim wrap should be about half an inch long.

After several coats of color preserver have been applied, two coats of varnish are brushed on butt wrap (and guide wraps) to complete the winding operation.

I hope you'll want to put an honest-to-gosh diamond wrap on your rod, but if the fish are hitting and you're in a hurry to get out there with them, there's an easier way to go. It's called butt-wind tape, and what it is is a flat tape of woven nylon about 3/32-inch wide, sold in three-yard lengths. It's available in several two-tone and solid colors from most of the catalog houses that sell rod-building components.

You can apply butt-wind tape over an underwrap just like a diamond wrap, or you can put it directly on the blank. Proceed as described for a diamond wrap by deciding how far up the rod shaft you want the tape to run, then mark half-inch increments along the shaft (both top and bottom) where the tape will intersect.

Run the tape through a weighted book to keep it under tension and tape the end of it just forward of the handle, exactly as described for the diamond wrap. Rotate the rod in the wrapping jig and spiral on the tape so that it passes over every other mark, both top and bottom. As you approach the handle, unwrap a turn of the masking tape (or wrap on another piece) and tape the loose end of the butt-wind tape in place. Cut off the butt-wind tape so that a little of it remains sticking out beyond the masking tape. Now lock in the butt-wind tape with an overwrap just as described for the diamond wrap. Just before the overwrap reaches the masking tape, peel off the tape and trim the butt-wind tape at a 45-degree angle about midway between the overwrap and the winding check. Complete the overwrap and the job is done.

BUTT-WIND TAPE

51

Applying Color Preserver and Varnish

With all your guide, butt, and trim windings completed, you're ready to apply the finish—color preserver and varnish.

Color preserver, as previously described, has a very thin consistency and soaks completely into the winding thread. I prefer to apply it with the tip of my index finger, but a small, stiff brush will work just as well. Simply wet the tip of your index finger with preserver, press it to the wrap, and rotate the rod as it is held in the wrapping jig. Spread any excess evenly with your finger, allow fifteen or twenty minutes for it to dry, and repeat two or three times. Allow the final coat of preserver to dry overnight before applying varnish.

As noted earlier, several different types of varnish and epoxy-type finishes are available. My preference, also as previously noted, is polyurethane-based varnish available from most catalog houses in one-ounce bottles. Apply at least three coats of varnish with a good quality brush, allowing ten to twelve hours of drying time between coats. It's important not to apply too heavy a coat of varnish at any one time, because the stuff has a nasty habit of running and sagging if you do. As you rotate the rod to apply varnish, be sure that all excess is removed and that no bubbles are left. Hang your rod vertically (by the tiptop) in a dust-free room while the varnish is drying.

With the final coat of varnish dry, you're ready to hang a reel on your new custom-built rod and take to the lake or stream. If you've done everything right (and I know you have), you now have a fishing tool that will give you pride and pleasure for many seasons to come.

6. Making Jigs
and Bucktails

Jigs are among the oldest lures around and one of the most effective for a broad variety of fish. For a good many years, they were all but forgotten by most fishermen. Then, about a decade ago, they came back with a vengeance. So much so, in fact, that some folks have been running about of late proclaiming things like, "If I had only one lure in my tacklebox, I'd want it to be a jig."

Fair enough. But my response to this is that if I had only one lure in my box, I'd take up golf. There's no question that jigs are proven fish-getters, and under the right circumstances will catch fish better than anything else. But I'll bet my hat, horse, and house cat that the biggest reason why some anglers think they're the all-purpose lure is their habit of chunking them into places they wouldn't dream of tossing a $3.67 crankbait.

And right there we have a couple of the greatest charms about jigs: they're cheap, and they're easy to make. Anyone with a couple of molds and a means of melting lead can crank out a year's supply in an afternoon after the grass is mowed or the snow shoveled. Moreover, the fantastic array of creepy critters (soft-body lures), plastic worms, and rubber skirts now available to dress them with has far expanded their usefulness. We're going to be talking more about that in a little while, but right now, let's hunker down and talk molding.

Making Your Own Molds

Years ago, before good commercial molds were available, I tried making molds from plaster of Paris. At the time, I was more interested in turning out heavy lead sinkers to use on trotlines. The process for making your own jig molds is essentially the same and fairly simple. Only thing is, it's slower and not quite as precise as using one of the excellent aluminum models now available from Do-It Corporation of Denver, Iowa. The good part about making your own molds, of course, is that your investment in time is offset by the *lack* of investment in cash.

To get started, save a couple of cardboard milk cartons. The half-gallon size works best. Then run over to the hardware store and get a

small-size (2½-pound) box of plaster of Paris. The $1.25 you spend will
be your only investment.

*Pin molds made of plaster of Paris are easy
assignments for the home craftsman following instructions provided in text.*

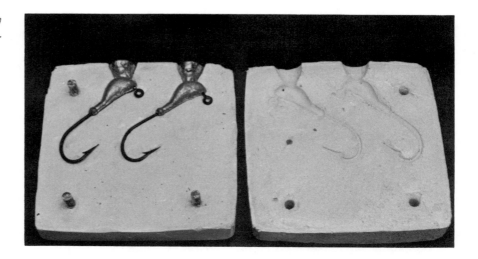

Cut off the bottom two inches of the milk carton and slit it at all
four corners. Now tape it back together. Take three good-size nails and
saw off the heads and points so that you have pins about an inch long.
File off one end of each of the pins to give it a rounded contour. Mix
up enough plaster of Paris to fill your milk carton about three-quarters
of an inch. Mix the plaster so that it pours easily and empty it into the
carton; smack the carton on your workbench a few times to remove any
air pockets. Wait several minutes for the plaster to begin to set up, then
impress your pins all the way in at three corners of the mold. About
one-half inch from the top of the mold, press in the jigs you want to
make until they are half in and half out of the plaster. Before you set
the jigs in the plaster, coat them with Pam or a similar cooking spray.
Now go fishing and let the plaster harden.

When you return to the workbench, spray Pam liberally on the bottom half of your mold (still in the milk carton), and pour in another
¾ inch or so of freshly mixed plaster. Go fishing again.

With the plaster fully set, pull the tape off the carton and open it
up. Gently separate the upper and lower halves of your pin mold, which,
if you've been listening carefully to your Uncle Jim, will be perfectly
formed. Remove the pattern jigs and use your pocketknife and a round
needle file to form sprue holes leading from the top of the mold down
into the jig cavities. The sprue holes should be slightly larger than those
used in aluminum molds, due to the nature of plaster.

Now, the final and most important step: Place the separated molds
in the oven (set at about 250 degrees Fahrenheit) for a couple of hours
to drive all the moisture out of the plaster. If you don't do this, they'll
spit lead all over the place, which—in addition to being dangerous—
makes it impossible to cast perfect jigs.

With your molds still warm, use C-clamps to hold them together and
pour in your lead (directions follow). If you prefer to buy your milk in
plastic jugs or you own your own cow, the carton you used for making

54

your first mold can be set aside and used repeatedly for making other molds for jigs or plastic worms. It's a time-tested procedure that'll work every time if you do it right.

Should you decide to forgo making your own molds and elect to go the simpler route of buying them, your first decision is what type or shapes of jig heads you want to make. Size isn't quite as important, because most of the commercial molds have cavities for three or four different sizes in the same configuration. Roundhead jigs, widely used for perch and walleye fishing in the Upper Midwest, have probably been around the longest. Bullet and lima-bean (Upperman) jigs have also been around quite a while, and Erie and dart (shad) jigs are excellent for the purposes for which they're intended. Because 90 percent of my fishing is for largemouth bass, I favor the banana jig made weedless by adding nylon fibers or a Y guard ahead of the hook. To my mind, it may well be the most versatile jig made.

Store-bought Molds and Other Equipment

Typical Jig Heads

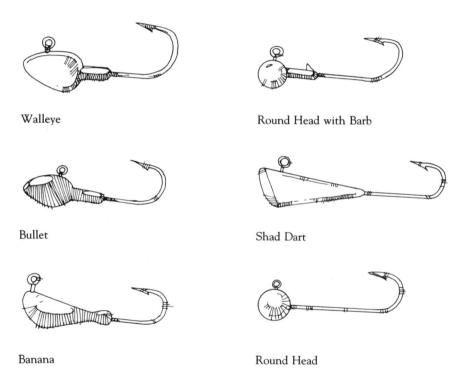

Walleye

Round Head with Barb

Bullet

Shad Dart

Banana

Round Head

No matter what kinds of jigs you want to make, chances are some mold maker has anticipated your need. Do-It Corporation alone lists some sixty mold models and, just in case you come up with a design no one has thought of before, also offers a blank model that lets you create your own design with router or Moto-Tool. Two basic types of molds are available: the pinned variety like those you make from plaster, or hinged. The pinned molds are a little cheaper, but they're slower to use. My preference is the hinged type with heat-dissipating wooden handles. Treat 'em right, and they're darned near foolproof.

Multiple-cavity, hinged molds made of aluminum, such as this one by Do-It Corporation, make it possible for the home craftsman to produce hundreds of jigs in a few hours.

Melting Lead

Melting lead obviously requires a heat source. Pure lead melts at about 620 degrees Fahrenheit, and alloyed lead at slightly higher temperatures. This obviously rules out the cheap little hotplates, though heavy-duty ones with variable controls will sometimes give you the temperature you need. The kitchen at our house is strictly off limits to me and my projects, and even if it weren't, I wouldn't dare melt lead on the kitchen stove. Besides the possibility of tipping the melted lead over and creating all sorts of problems, lead fumes are potentially toxic. Melting lead anywhere in the proximity of where food will be prepared is asking for trouble. A propane stove, preferably out in the carport or garage, is much to be preferred.

A two- or three-burner tabletop stove, fueled with either natural gas or propane, is ideal for melting lead. Though no longer widely available, tabletop stoves can often be picked up at flea markets or garage sales for a few dollars.

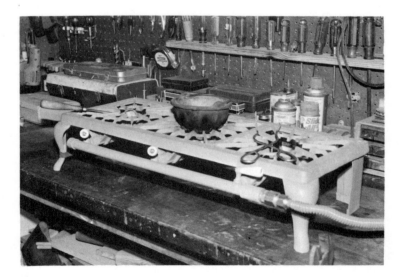

If you use an external heat source, you'll also need a cast-iron melting pot, and a ladle or bottom-pour dipper. The latter is a lot easier to use, and eliminates the problem of imperfectly formed jigs caused by slag inclusions. Small, relatively inexpensive electric "hot pots" suitable for melting three or four pounds of lead at a time are fine for jig casting, and are available from several catalog houses, including Cabela's, Sportsman's Supply, and Bass Pro Shops. Although these have their own pouring lips, I find it much easier to use them in conjunction with a bottom-pour dipper.

One step up the ladder are the large-capacity, bottom-pour electric furnaces with calibrated heat controls. Popularized by Lee, Lyman, and other suppliers for the hand-loading fraternity, these units are increasingly popular with tackle crafters as well. The one I use for a variety of assignments is made by Santa Anita Engineering Company (SAECO) and has a twelve-pound lead capacity. Its major advantage for tackle making is its ability to digest fairly large chunks of scrap lead. The great advantage of bottom-pour furnaces is that they completely eliminate the bother of pouring slag, and measure predetermined amounts of lead into the mold.

Bottom-pour electric furnaces, like this model from SAECO, simplify jig-molding procedures when hinged aluminum molds are used.

No one disagrees that pure (soft) lead is best for molding jigs. It pours better than alloyed lead (lead with varying amounts of tin and antimony added), fills the cavities faster and more reliably, and melts faster. I personally think the necessity of obtaining high-priced pure lead has been considerably overstated by mold makers and other authorities. The simple fact is that if you heat alloyed lead to a fairly high (say, 800 degrees Fahrenheit) temperature and hold it there for about thirty minutes, a large percentage of the tin and antimony will separate out and float to the surface, where it can be skimmed off along with the slag or dross. Hand loaders, who *want* a harder, alloyed lead for their molded bullets, flux their lead to prevent this very thing from happening. I've never had too much difficulty obtaining scrap lead from a variety of

Working With Lead

57

sources—wheel weights, Linotype slugs, cable sheathing, roof flashing, and so forth—and have never encountered any problems in its use.

One minor problem you do encounter when using scrap lead is that it may emit a fair amount of smoke and fumes. This is why I usually pick a nice day and do my melting out on the patio or in the carport. You can burn off smoke created by scrap lead by holding a propane torch with spreader head over your furnace or melting pot until the impurities are eliminated. I usually melt all my scrap lead at one time and pour it up into a four-cavity ingot mold (also made by SAECO). This way, I have a good supply of pure lead in bite-size chunks available when I begin molding jigs or spinnerbaits.

Before using your new mold, use a candle or kitchen matches to smoke the cavities. This one-time operation will help keep your casts from sticking in the mold. Also, if you are using a hinged mold, spray a little WD-40 on the hinges before you start molding, and at frequent intervals thereafter. It's also necessary to heat your mold before you begin casting. When I'm using an aluminum mold, I simply place it on top of my furnace as the lead gets hot. If I'm using a plaster mold, I stick it in the oven for a few minutes at 250 degrees Fahrenheit. You can also heat an aluminum mold with a spreader head on a propane torch, or by pouring a few cavities full of lead without the hooks in place. If you use a torch to heat your mold, be careful not to overdo it; you can warp the mold if you get it too hot.

Dip your ladle or dipper into the melted lead and let it heat for a few minutes, then pour your first cavity. If you are using the bottom-pour dipper that I advocate, simply hold the mold on its side, fit the sprue hole of the mold over the spout on the dipper, and tilt them upright together until the sprue hole is filled. Don't be timid about the speed with which you do this: allowing the lead to cool in the cavity before all of it is filled will lead to wrinkled castings. You'll soon learn how much lead to have in your dipper to fill the cavity and sprue hole perfectly every time.

The procedure is even easier if you are using a bottom-pour furnace. In this instance, the mold's sprue hole is simply fitted over the pour spout on the bottom of the furnace, and the lead-release lever tripped to fill the cavity. A brief period of experimentation will tell you where to adjust the trip release for a perfect pour.

I seldom pour more than one or two cavities at a time, as the lead solidifies almost instantly, and the finished jig head is ready to be dumped atop your work surface. If the jig fails to release when the mold is opened, a light tap on the top of your workbench, or with a wooden mallet, will do the job. Remember that the castings are too hot to handle with bare hands for several minutes after they come out of the mold, so if you have to handle them, do it with a pair of pliers or heavy gloves.

As you near the end of your casting quota for the day but before you shut down your furnace, remove the sprues and return them to the pot for remelting. Side-cutter pliers are commonly used to remove sprues, but if you're using pure lead, a cleaner separation will usually result if you twist them off with pliers. If you use side-cutters, you'll likely need to smooth the top of the jig head with a few passes of a file before priming and painting.

There's not a whole lot to be said about hook selection as it pertains to jig making, except to observe that if you try to use a size or style much different from that recommended by the mold manufacturer, you're going to have problems. Pick too large a size and your mold won't close, too small a size and you'll get flashing (lead overrun). The main thing to watch for is that the hook eye fits perfectly into the cavity provided for it. Hooks with eyes that are too big can restrict the flow of lead and cause incomplete castings.

Mold makers specify proper hook sizes and styles in the instruction booklets accompanying their molds, and some of them even cast the sizes right into their molds. So if you go wrong, you just ain't listening up like you should. Catalog houses, to their credit, are usually quite specific in stating the recommended hooks for each mold they carry and equally diligent in their ability to supply same. Local tackle shops, unfortunately, aren't always so mindful of their customers' needs. I once purchased a mold at a tackle shop in my area, only to discover there wasn't a hook in the house to fit it. Needless, perhaps, to recount, the mold was promptly returned to the shelf and I placed a phone call to a midwestern catalog house. Nowadays, Uncle Jim admonishes his fishin' buddies to lay by a goodly supply of hooks when ordering their molds.

Jig-hook sizes vary all over the map, but two styles—Aberdeen and O'Shaughnessy—are specified for about 90 percent of the jigs I'm familiar with. Of these two styles, the Aberdeens are by far the most widely used. These little hooks are made from relatively soft wire and their bends are rounded rather than forged (flattened). This allows them to straighten out and pull free of underwater obstructions; then they can be rebent with sharp-nosed pliers when retrieved. They're available in either bronze or gold finish. I tend to prefer the latter because they seem to resist corrosion a little better.

The O'Shaughnessy is a big, gutsy hook made from harder steel, and its bends are forged. They'll usually break off before bending. Most O'Shaughnessy hooks used for freshwater fishing are also bronzed or gold finished, while those used for salt water are cadmium plated. The catalog houses are now also listing a stainless-steel O'Shaughnessy available at substantially higher prices. The way I lose jigs, this seems to be gilding the lily a bit.

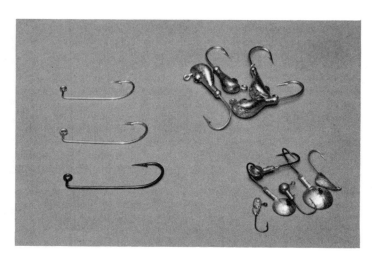

Jig hooks, such as these O'Shaughnessy hooks in sizes 2/0, 3/0, and 4/0 (top to bottom at left), are the usual choice for large jigs, such as banana jigs (top right). Smaller jigs (lower right) usually call for lighter Aberdeen hooks.

Priming and Painting

There are several schools of thought when it comes to painting jig heads. One holds that it's the dressing that does all the work and that heads should be as inconspicuous as possible. You'll never find anything except flat black or unpainted heads in these fellows' tackle boxes. Another school holds that the head should complement whatever dressing is selected. That is, an orange-skirted tail should take an orange-painted head, and so on. Yet another school holds that the jig head should be as flashy or fishlike as possible. You'll find these fellows fishing with fluorescent colors, painted eyes, and red gill stripes on the heads of their jigs.

Me, I find myself somewhere in between schools two and three, but I'm not a bit reluctant to go to flat black heads if another guy in the boat is catching fish with them. I'm not ambivalent; I just can't make up my mind. The upshot is that my jig box weighs about twenty pounds because it's filled with jigs in a variety of sizes and colors.

One thing you should do, whatever school of thought you subscribe to, is neutralize and prime your jig heads shortly after you mold them. Lead oxidizes, and under poor conditions can build up a cruddy mess that will rot your dressing and rust your hooks. The easiest way of neutralizing jigs is simply to dip them in vinegar and let them air-dry overnight on a paper towel. When they're dry, prime them with an ordinary primer paint such as is used on auto bodies. Alternatively, you can buy a neutral-base primer such as that made by Weber Tackle Company of Stevens Point, Wisconsin, and forget about the vinegar dip.

Priming done, you're ready to paint your jigs. Dipping, spraying, and brushing all have their advantages. Dipping is fast and gives the best coverage, but it tends to clog the hook eye and little globs of paint sometimes form on the nose of your jig. Spraying also provides good coverage if you take your time and apply the paint in two or three light coats, rather than a single heavy one that invariably causes runs. Spraying has the disadvantage of getting some paint on the exposed shank of the hook. While this probably poses no great disability from a fish's viewpoint, it looks a little messy. If you want to spray paint your jig heads—either for the primer or finish coats—check out the photo of a painting box. This simple device will make the job a lot neater.

Paint primer can be sprayed on several jigs at one time by using a painting box rigged as shown. Lead heads should be neutralized with vinegar unless a neutral-base primer is used.

Hand (brush) painting is the most precise—you get the paint where you want it and nowhere else. It's also the slowest, and it's a little hard to get good coverage with a single coat. My usual approach is to brush on a coat of primer and a coat of paint before tying my jigs, then add another coat of paint after the tying is done. This is admittedly a labor-intensive method, but it's the best way to put a bunch of good-looking jigs in your tackle box.

Solid colors in black, red, yellow, and white are the most popular, depending largely on what breed of fish you're angling for. The flashiest colors are the fluorescents in yellow, red, and orange. Looking back, I'd have to say I've taken more fish on black, but that's likely because I've fished that color most often for largemouth bass. If I did more crappie fishing, I'd certainly opt for white or yellow, and some little roundhead jigs in fluorescent red performed as advertised on Wisconsin walleye last summer. I can't honestly say that jigs with eyes (or gill stripes) painted on them catch more fish; I've never been able to tell much difference. But it takes only a second to dab on eyes using the head of a small finishing nail, so I usually do it. Yellow and red are the most popular colors for eyes.

Any number of good paints are available for painting jig heads. I've used auto-body enamel in both aerosol cans and little applicator bottles with good results. Illinois Bronze Company makes a good hobby enamel, and Testor's gloss enamel (the kind recommended for kids eight and over) stays on about as well as anything I've tried. The specially formulated plug lacquer sold by Netcraft works fine on jigs as well. No matter what paint you use, occasional touch-ups are going to be required. If you want to eliminate these touch-ups altogether, coat your painted heads with one of the epoxy-type plastic finishes, such as those made by Behr Process Corp., which are available at most hardware stores. Another good permanent coating is Plasti Dip, intended primarily for coating tool handles. It's available in four colors as well as a clear finish. Unlike epoxy, it requires no mixing.

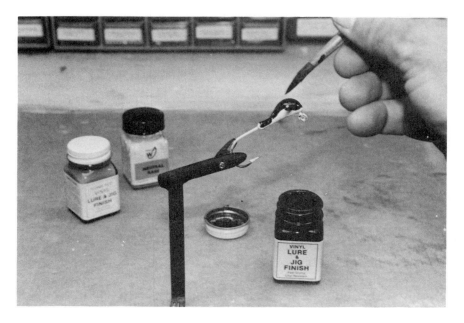

Applied over primer, any good enamel will coat jig heads adequately. For best chip resistance, though, special vinyl-based paint is preferable.

61

Drying of paint can be accelerated by using a blowdryer.

Maximum chip resistance is obtained by dipping jig heads in an epoxy-type plastic finish or single-coat plastic product, such as Plasti Dip.

Dressing and Tying Jigs

Compared with tying flies, jigs are a snap. They can be dressed with any number of different materials—bucktail and other natural hair, tinsel, living rubber in ready-made skirts or strips, and that old crappie fisherman's favorite, maribou feathers. One of my favorites, because it's so easy to use, is Dynel Fishair, a synthetic hair available from Netcraft and Tackle Crafters, among others. A sampler pack that contains ten different colors will keep you in business for several tying sessions.

No matter what material you use—and eventually you'll likely want to try them all—the method of tying is the same. The only tools you'll need are a fly-tying vise of bench-mounted locking pliers, a spool of nylon thread (size D or larger), a bobbin, a small pair of scissors, a bottle of head cement, and a sharp knife.

To get started, secure your jig in a vise and make several wraps over the jig collar with your thread to hold it in place. Snip off the tag end of the thread and make one complete wrap down the length of the collar to form a cushion for the dressing. As you reverse your wrapping direction back up the collar, add a small pinch of hair or feathers and secure it with two or three wraps. Continue adding dressing and wrapping in this manner until the entire collar is skirted. Now, make one more complete wrap of the entire collar and add two half-hitches to hold the whole works in place. Use your knife or fly-tying scissors to

With underwrap made down length of jig collar, wrap in pieces of Fishair or other dressing a few strands at a time. Here, acetate floss is used in place of winding thread.

With dressing tied in all around jig collar, fly-tying scissors are used to snip off excess hair next to head.

trim off excess dressing in front of the wrap (next to the head). Continue wrapping until the forward ends of the dressing (the ones you've just trimmed) are covered. Tie off with several half-hitches, cut off the thread as closely as possible with your scissors, and add a few drops of head cement to seal. There. You've got it done.

There's a really nifty product, available from Netcraft, that substitutes for nylon thread. It's called acetate floss, and it's available in several basic colors that more or less match the color of your dressing. You wrap it on exactly as you do nylon thread, but after you're through wrapping you secure it with a special solvent (supplied with the floss) that fuses the whole thing together. You can paint over the wrapping with enamel, but it tends to blister lacquer.

63

Special solvent is applied to acetate floss to fuse wrapping. Enamel, but not lacquer, can be used to paint wrapping after solvent dries.

Using the method I've described, it's possible to use two or more different colors, or even different types of material, for dressing your jigs. I frequently tie in different colors of tinsel or living rubber and have experimented with various combinations of hair, tinsel, and feathers. Combinations look good, but my experience has been that they often don't run as well as dressings of a single material.

Jigs dressed with living rubber and used in combination with pork rind or soft-bodied lures such as plastic grubs and worms have become mighty popular in the bass-fishing fraternity. I go through a pile of them every year. The easiest way to dress a jig is simply to slip a rubber skirt over the jig collar and start fishing it. The skirts, in a rainbow of colors, sell for about thirty cents apiece in bulk and several cents more at your local tackle shop. A cheaper and somewhat more flexible way to go is to buy filament rubber in long, pre-slit strips and tie it on yourself. It takes a tad more doing, but the results (and savings) are worth the effort.

The same nylon thread you use for tying on other materials works okay with filament rubber, but I've found it easier to use fine (28-gauge), soft wire. Filament rubber is available in small, medium, and large thicknesses, but my advice is to go with the small—it "breathes" or undulates much better in the water.

Start by cutting off a length of filament rubber about twice as long as you want your finished skirt to be. Position the strip so that the jig collar is at its middle and wrap it around the collar. Now secure it with a tight wrap of wire, twist the wire around itself a couple of times, and finish by wrapping around the collar half a dozen times.

64

With living-rubber strip positioned on jig collar midway along its length, wrap several strands of light-gauge wire around the collar as described in text.

Twist the ends of the wire together several times and trim off the excess with side-cutters. Bend the twisted ends down against the jig body. Now, stretch the rubber strip away from the jig body and cut it with scissors close to the end; this releases the pre-slit strands. The only step remaining is to trim the strands to their desired length. You've got yourself a rubber-skirted jig about half the price of a factory-made skirt tail.

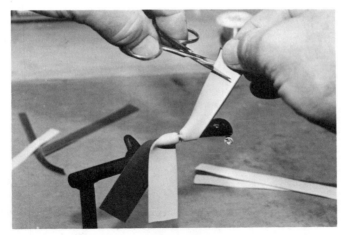

Stretch the strip and trim with scissors, causing it to separate into individual filaments.

Finished jig has a rubber skirt at about half the price of a factory-made skirt tail.

65

Thoughts on Weedless Jigs

Although I don't advocate them for walleye or panfish, I much prefer to do my bass fishing with jigs made weedless by the addition of plastic or nylon-fiber weed guards. I consider these much superior to the bent-wire guards I've seen from time to time. The use of plastic weed guards requires that your jigs be molded for the purpose and of a configuration that will accommodate the insertion of guards. As noted earlier, I think the weedless banana jig is a classic design.

Weed guards made of nylon fiber come in black and clear. I use black guards on black and other dark-colored jigs, and clear ones with lighter colors. The nylon fibers are glued together in little bunches designed to fit the holes molded into weedless-style jigs. The guards are glued into place (Duco cement works fine for the purpose) either before or after you paint your jig head. Another type of weed guard, known as a Y guard because of its configuration, has been just as effective as the fiber type in preventing hang-ups for me, and I think that perhaps these guards interfere with hooking ability even less than nylon fiber does. They also are glued into the hole molded in the jig head.

After allowing the cement to cure for thirty minutes or so, use a pair of tin snips or heavy-duty scissors to trim the guard diagonally so that the longest fibers extend just a tad beyond the point of your hook. Y guards, of course, have only two arms, but these should also be trimmed so that they extend just past the hook point. I emphasize this because I've fished with some fellows who didn't trim the guards and then wondered why they were missing so many strikes. To intelligent types like you and me, it's obvious that any lure that's totally snag-proof is also totally fish-proof. Nobody said it was a perfect world we fish in.

Nylon-fiber weed guards should be trimmed diagonally so that longest filaments extend just past point of hook.

7. Spinnerbaits and Buzzbaits

When we talk about spinnerbaits, we're really talking about at least three different breeds of cat. First are the in-line spinners, such as the Mepps and Rooster Tail, that have been around for years. Next are the safety-pin spinnerbaits that came along a couple of decades ago. And finally, there are the buzzbaits, beloved of southern bass anglers.

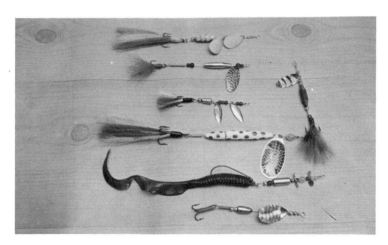

In-line spinnerbaits have been around for years. They are popular because of the wide variety of designs possible and because they are deadly for many species of fish.

Safety-pin spinnerbaits and buzzbaits have proved their effectiveness on predatory game fish, such as black bass and northern pike. Clockwise from upper left: Tandem-blade spinnerbait with rubber skirt; tandem-blade spinnerbait with Fishair; buzzbait with open (pinched) line tie; buzzbait with closed (looped) line tie; and single-blade spinnerbait.

67

What all three of these lures have in common, besides their uncommon ability to catch fish, are blades that spin or revolve and act as fish attractors. In the case of buzzbaits, the delta-shaped blades revolve around an axis formed by an upper shaft. Buzzbaits are exclusively top-water lures, in-line spinners are essentially sinking lures, and safety-pin spinners can be fished up or down. Jigs are also used in combination with spinners, adding another dimension to this already versatile lure.

There must be at least a dozen different kinds of spinner blades in fairly common use today, and likely a few more some angler down in Louisiana or Florida is keeping secret. The hands-down favorite for use with safety-pin spinnerbaits is the Colorado blade, a relatively wide (in relation to its length) blade that revolves easily and imparts lift to the lure. Indiana blades are similar in design, but more narrow in relation to length. They're commonly used with in-line spinners, but also with safety-pin spinnerbaits when less lift is desired. Another popular blade for use with in-line spinnerbaits is the willowleaf. As its name implies, it's more elongated than either the Colorado or Indiana blade.

A fourth type of blade, immortalized by Mepps, is the French spinner. Similar to the Indiana in overall shape, it is characterized by a raised center dome on its convex side that causes water to cavitate and create a bubbling action. Some claim it's primarily responsible for the uncanny fish-getting ability of the Mepps line of spinnerbaits.

Other types of blades common to in-line spinners are the ripple, swing, and June bug. Swing blades are sort of a fat willow-leaf design, while ripple blades have essentially the same overall shape but are crinkled like those fancy potato chips. The June bug has a midsection that pushes out to form an arm that fits on the shaft of an in-line spinner and eliminates the need for a clevis.

All spinner blades come in a variety of sizes and colors, including polished brass and nickel. Other popular colors include black, red, yellow, white, and chartreuse. They're also available in metal flake and combination colors.

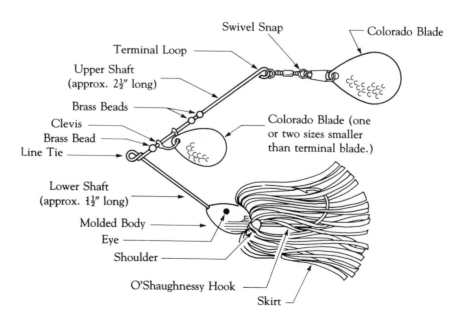

Spinnerbait Construction

TANDEM BLADE

Swivel Snap — Colorado Blade

Terminal Loop

Upper Shaft
(approx. 2½" long)

Brass Beads

Clevis

Brass Bead

Line Tie

Colorado Blade (one
or two sizes smaller
than terminal blade.)

Lower Shaft
(approx. 1½" long)

Molded Body

Eye

Shoulder

O'Shaughnessy Hook

Skirt

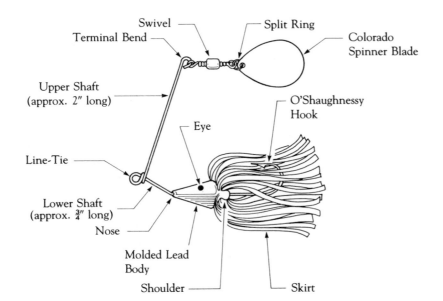

Spinnerbait Construction
SINGLE BLADE

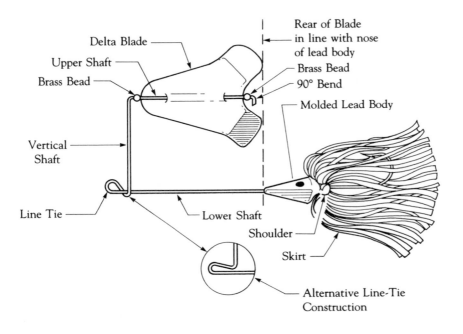

Buzzbait Construction

It's fairly easy to make your own blades from sheet brass, but they're so cheap to buy that it hardly seems worthwhile. Repainting tarnished and battered blades is something else again, especially with the luminous paints that are available today. Another thing I sometimes dress up my battered blades with is the diffractive-prism, pressure-sensitive tape sold by Cabela's and others. A number of designs are available.

The techniques used in making safety-pin spinnerbaits are similar to those used in making jigs. Both involve molding lead and, usually skirts of some kind to cover the hooks. An added dimension is involved with

Making Safety-Pin Spinnerbaits

spinnerbaits, however, in that wire forming also comes into play. Inexpensive wire-forming tools are available from most of the catalog houses, or you can go whole hog and—for about $40—buy the outstanding Professional Spinner Maker available from Cabela's. The latter uses three different-size heads for various sizes of wire, and this is its great advantage over the cheaper models.

Components needed to make safety-pin spinnerbaits include brass beads, clevises, swivels, Colorado blades, molded head with wire shaft, and rubber skirts or other dressing.

If safety-pin spinners are all you plan to make, you can do the job just fine with a wire-forming tool you make yourself. Just take a length of 1-by-2-inch hardwood (the kind you get from packing crates) and drive a couple of closely spaced six-penny nails into it. Now, cut off the heads of the nails about an inch from the board and round off the stubs with a file. Add another single nail for simple bends and you're done. You'll be surprised how many wire-forming chores—from simple bends to double angles—you can perform with this tool when it's clamped to the top of your workbench.

Three types of wire-forming tools. (Top) This tool, carried by hardware stores, is too large for most tackle-making chores. Nails driven into a length of hardwood (center) make the best tool for forming spinnerbaits and buzzbaits. (Bottom) Made by Worth Tackle, this tool will perform most wire-bending chores associated with making in-line spinnerbaits.

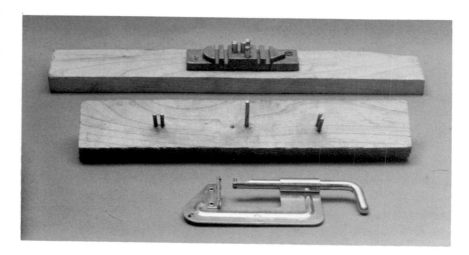

For casting the lead heads of your safety-pin spinners, you can make your own pin molds from plaster of Paris using the same procedure described in the preceding chapters on jigs. Alternatively (and preferably), you can buy Do-It Corporation's hinged aluminum model made specially for spinnerbaits. If you elect to try casting spinnerbaits in homemade molds, be advised that it's somewhat more difficult than molding jigs, because both hook and wire shaft must be held in place while the lead is being poured. I've done it, but it ain't easy.

Hooks of appropriate types and sizes are your next consideration. Safety-pin spinnerbaits are noted for their ability to get into and out of all kinds of tight places, so it follows that tough O'Shaughnessy hooks rather than easily bent Aberdeens should be your choice of hook. Do-It's four-cavity mold specifies size 2/0 and 3/0 hooks for heads that range from 5/16 oz. to 3/8 oz. If you're of the "bigger hook-bigger fish" school, size 4/0 hooks also work.

Wire type and size are also important. Do-It recommends a .040″-diameter single-strand wire for its spinnerbait mold. Stainless-steel leader wire of this size is available from several of the catalog houses. (Netcraft lists a quarter-pound coil of .041″-diameter leader wire in either nickel or brown finish for $2.85.) You can also buy leader wire precut to various lengths. This has the advantage of not requiring straightening, but it's more expensive than coiled wire and I never seem to have the proper length on hand when I want it.

You can make a simple wire-straightening device by sawing (use a backsaw if you have one) a straight groove in a piece of 1-by-2-inch hardwood about a foot long. Cut the coiled wire to the lengths you need, then pull it through the groove and straighten by hand as you pull it out. This avoids the kinks and nicks you can get when using pliers to straighten the wire.

Although I concede that stainless-steel wire is preferable, I've used plain old spring (piano) wire with good results for years. Of course, it will rust if you don't wipe it off after a fishing trip, but so will lots of other stuff in a tackle box.

How long should your lengths of wire be? Well, it depends on personal choice and the type of spinnerbaits you're making. But I've found 5½ inches or so about right for single-blade lures and 7 inches long enough for tandem-blade rigs. One thing is for sure: It's a whole lot easier to trim off a little wire in the final manufacturing stage than to add on, so don't skimp on wire length.

With your wire cut to length and straightened, fit about a quarter-inch of it into your wire former and bend a loop. Pass the eye of the hook over the bend and squeeze it shut with pliers. Place the wire with hook attached in the cavity of your heated mold and pour in the lead. When we were talking about jig making in the last chapter, I spoke highly of the bottom-pour electric furnace. Such a device still serves well for melting your lead, but because of the wire shaft sticking out of the top of spinnerbait molds, you can't use its bottom-pour capability. Instead, use a ladle or bottom-pour dipper to pour lead into the mold. It takes only a few seconds longer.

My practice is to mold a couple dozen heads, cut the sprues and return them to the furnace for remelting, then shut down the furnace be-

For molding spinnerbait heads, single-strand wire is bent and looped through eye of hook, usually an O'Shaughnessy.

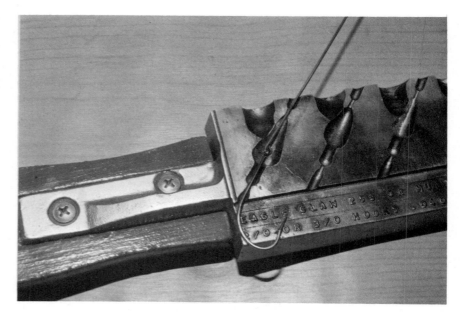

Bottom-pour dipper is used to pour lead into sprue hole of hinged aluminum mold.

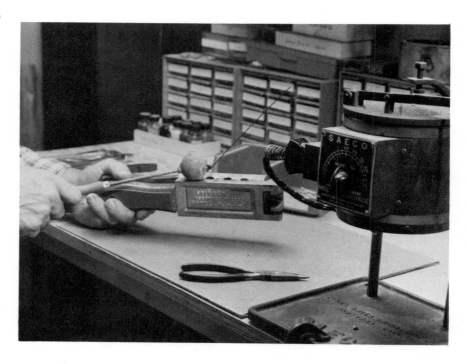

fore beginning my wire-forming operation. Depending on personal choice, come out about an inch from the nose of the head to bend the line tie on a single-blade spinnerbait, and about 1¾ inches for a tandem-blade spinner. It will help to take a look at the commercially made spinnerbaits in your tackle box and observe their dimensions.

Using the single post (nail) of your homemade wire former, bend a wire loop completely around so that the resulting upper shaft extends from the lower shaft at about a 30-degree angle. This loop forms your line tie. Now bend the lower shaft (wire) where it enters the lead head to an angle of about 30 degrees. Make sure that the bottom of the terminal spinner blade clears the point of the hook.

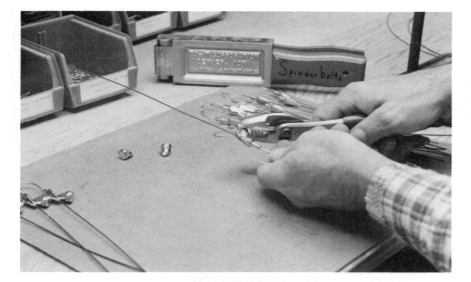

After a number of heads have been molded, sprues are trimmed and tossed back into the melting furnace.

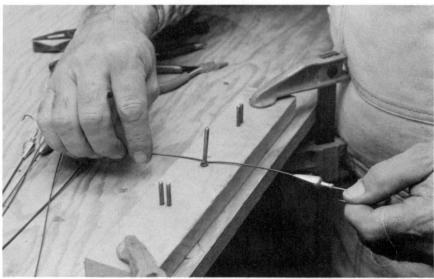

Begin wire-forming operations by bending tie line in the wire shaft. See text for specifics.

Wire is bent around itself to complete line tie; note that shaft now points in the same direction as, and is parallel to, the point of the hook.

If you are making a single-blade lure, now is the time to bend a loop in the end of the upper shaft that will hold the blade. Be sure the loop is bent *down* (toward the hook), so it won't hang up on underwater obstructions. Add a swivel (size 5 or 6 is about right) and squeeze the loop shut. If you're making tandem-blade lures, slide a couple of brass beads onto the upper shaft immediately above the line tie, add a clevis (size 3) with blade attached, a couple more beads, and then bend the terminal loop to hold the rear blade. Most makers prefer to have the forward blade a size or two smaller than the terminal blade. For example, if the terminal blade selected is size 5, the forward blade should be a size 3 or 4. The theory is that enough water will bypass the smaller forward blade to provide good action for the larger terminal blade.

If tandem-blade spinnerbait is being made, terminal loop is bent after beads, clevis, and forward blade have been placed on shaft.

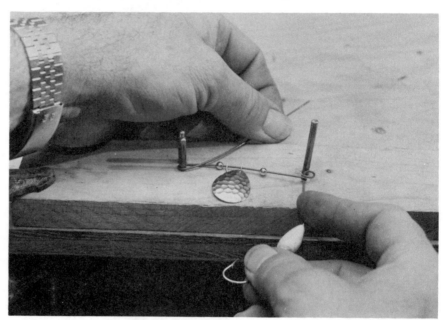

Terminal loop is bent after barrel swivel has been placed on shaft.

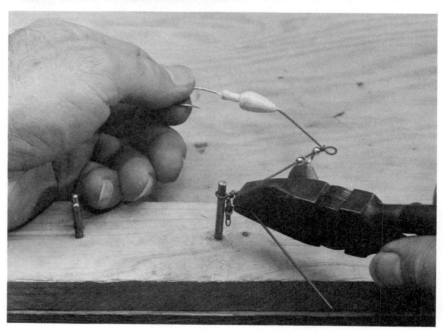

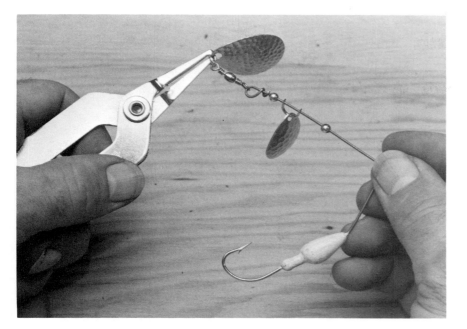

Split-ring pliers are used to add rear blade to swivel with split ring.

This may sound like trivia, but it's worth our while to devote a few words to the choice of clevises. You wouldn't think a simple little thing like a clevis—merely a U-shaped piece of metal—could create problems. But believe me, if you select the wrong size, it most certainly will. Clevises come in sizes 0 through 4, with size 4 being the largest. Make sure the size you select has holes large enough to revolve freely on the shaft, and that the blade has plenty of room between the bottom of the clevis and the shaft of the lure. Also, there are two types of clevises in common use—*stirrup* and *folded.* The stirrup type, in my experience, gives superior blade action, but the folded clevises are likely a tad stronger. The best advice I can give you is to order clevises in sizes 1 through 4, then select the size that visual observation tells you is best suited to the project at hand.

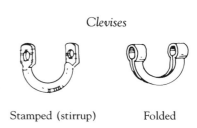

Clevises

Stamped (stirrup)   Folded

Final step before adding rubber skirt or other dressing is to paint the lead head. Note that neutral-base primer has already been brushed on.

Making Buzzbaits

Looking at a buzzbait, you wouldn't think any self-respecting fish would give it a second glance. On the contrary, they can be deadly to top-feeding largemouth bass, and I've also taken smallmouths and northern pike on them. The manufacture of buzzbaits is very similar to the methods used for making safety-pin spinnerbaits, but there *are* differences.

Components needed to make buzzbaits include aluminum rivets (not essential), brass beads, delta blades, molded head with wire shaft, and rubber skirts or other dressing.

The first, and perhaps primary, difference is in the size of wire selected for the shaft. While .040"-diameter leader wire is a good choice for spinnerbaits, it's not quite heavy enough to support the more violent action of delta blades used on buzzbaits. These blades, which derive their name from the fact that they resemble the fourth letter of the Greek alphabet, come in several sizes and designs. All, however, are designed to fit over the upper shaft of the bait, which acts as an axis upon which the blade rotates. The holes in most of these blades are made to fit over a wire shaft of .050"-diameter or slightly larger. It's difficult to find leader wire in diameters this large, but spring (piano) wire of this size is readily available.

The lengths of wire used for buzzbaits must be substantially longer (by about 3 inches) than those used for spinnerbaits. I've found that 8½ inches is a good length. Again, it's easier to trim than to add.

Some buzzbaits are made with lead heads molded in a flattened (skimmer) configuration, rather than the bullet shape common to spinnerbaits. The idea behind the skimmer design is that it provides more lift for a top-water lure such as the buzzbait. Do-It Corporation makes a mold for this type of head that they call their buzz-spin model. There may be some logic to the skimmer design, but I've used and been happy with bullet-shaped heads on buzzbaits for quite some time. If you want to go this route, the Do-It mold for spinnerbaits will work well for buzzbait molding as well. All that's required is to enlarge slightly with a round needle file the wire hole in the larger (⅜-oz.) cavity of the Do-It mold. This doesn't negate the use of the cavity for .040"-diameter spinnerbait wire, and it allows the mold to close tightly when .050″-diameter wire is used for buzzbaits. From there, proceed just as you would for molding spinnerbaits.

When you begin your wire-forming operations, measure out two to three inches from the nose of the head to make the line-tie bend. The exact length will depend on what size delta blade you are using; the important thing is to position the back of the blade about one-half inch ahead of the head. You can make a complete bend for the line tie as with spinnerbaits, or a pinched bend that comes partway down to the lower shaft before heading up again. Either way, come up from the lower shaft about an inch (the exact measurement will again depend on the size of your delta blade) and make a right-angle (90-degree) bend in the wire. At this juncture, the wire forming the upper shaft will point back toward the point of the hook.

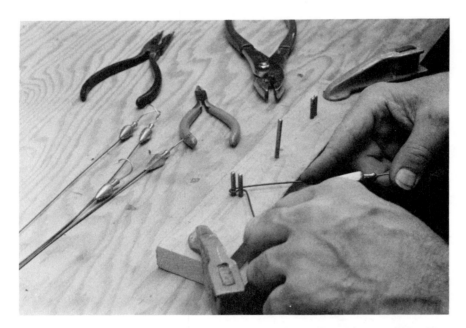

Begin wire-forming operations by bending a pinched line tie (as shown here) or a looped line tie.

A second, 90-degree bend is made in shaft about an inch above the line tie.

Now fit a brass bead over the upper shaft, followed by the delta blade, followed by another bead or aluminum rivet. Bend the end of the wire down toward the lower shaft in another 90-degree bend to hold the blade in place, and the operation is complete. The upper and lower shafts of a buzzbait should be more or less parallel. Most anglers fine-tune the upper shaft of their buzzbaits while they are out of the water to make them run deeper or more shallow. A slight upward bend will impart a little more lift to your lure and, some maintain, cause it to cavitate a bit more. Try it and see.

Due to size of delta blade, it's best to paint the lead head of a buzzbait before the blade is fitted on the shaft.

Upper shaft accommodates, in order of assembly, a brass bead, the delta blade, and an aluminum rivet or second brass bead.

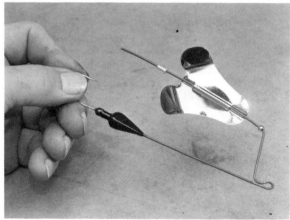

Ninety-degree bend is made in end of upper shaft, and wire clipped off as shown.

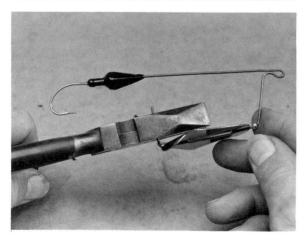

78

Completed buzzbait after rubber skirt has been added.

Any dressing that's used for jigs can also be used for safety-pin spinner-baits and buzzbaits. I've used tinsel and Fishair with good results, but as a practical matter, rubber skirts are the material of choice 90 percent of the time. Many anglers also use rubber (plastic) grubs, either in combination with rubber skirts or alone. Three-inch grubs with straight or twister tails work well, and I've also used pork-rind strips with success. Some folks swear by trailer hooks used with spinnerbaits for short-striking bass, but I've never found they put any more fish on my stringer.

Dressing Safety-Pin Spinners and Buzzbaits

I think in-line spinners of one sort or another have been around about as long as the casting rod; at least I can't remember a time when I didn't have a few of them in my tackle box. Just about every fish that swims has been taken on them, and for my money they are the best lures made for consistently catching smallmouth bass. The one problem that in-line spinners ever presented—casting distance—was eliminated with the advent of spinning tackle.

Making In-Line Spinners

In-line spinners, for all their effectiveness and versatility, essentially consist of nothing more than a piece of wire with a line tie on one end, a hook on the other, and a spinner blade in between. To this essential combination is added an assortment of brass or lead bodies, beads of brass and plastic, short lengths of plastic tubing, and just about anything else that strikes your fancy. Hooks, which can be singles, doubles, or trebles, are dressed with hair, tinsel, feathers, and various soft-bodied (plastic) lures such as worms, grubs, and minnows.

Stainless-steel wire shafts can be purchased in precut lengths ranging from 3 to 7 inches. Wire sizes used for in-line spinners commonly range from .025 to .030 inch in diameter, depending on the size of the lure to be formed. Precut shafts are often supplied with one end (the line tie) already looped, and if you don't plan to invest in a good wire-forming device, this is a good way to go. As with making safety-pin spinner-baits, the most economical approach is to purchase coiled leader wire and cut it to length.

Several of the catalog houses carry lure-making kits. The kit put together by Worth Tackle contains everything necessary to make twenty-five or more lures. Cabela's current catalog lists the Worth kit for $21.95. Considering that factory-made lures of comparable quality list for $1.75

79

to $2.50 each, it's not a bad price. The Worth kit contains a simple wire-forming tool, paint, shafts, and an assortment of blades and bodies. Starting from scratch and buying all your components in bulk, you can make in-line spinnerbaits for about twenty-five cents apiece.

With this as a prelude, let's move to the workbench and make up several lures using coiled leader wire and a variety of components. Cutting and straightening the wire, just as we did when we were making safety-pin spinnerbaits, is the first order of business. If you want to do most of your wire cutting at one time, four-inch and six-inch lengths will serve as shafts for all but the largest in-line spinnerbaits.

Now begin your wire-forming operation by bending a line tie (the loop to which your fishing line will be attached) in one end of the shaft. It's possible to do this using the simple nail-in-wood device described earlier in combination with pliers. But you'll get a much tighter and stronger twist, and be better satisfied with the results, if you use one of the wire-forming tools made by Cabela's or Worth. Only two twists around the shaft are required to form a closed (wrapped-end) loop, so make your bend about half an inch from the end of the shaft. To run true, the shaft must be perfectly aligned with the line-tie loop, so pause now to inspect your work and straighten with pliers if necessary.

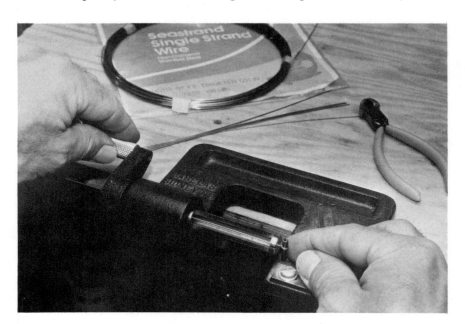

Using .026-inch-diameter stainless-steel wire and Cabela's Professional Spinner Maker, author bends line-tie loop to begin in-line spinnerbait manufacturing operation.

Begin constructing the lure by placing a couple of attractor (usually red plastic) beads on the shaft immediately behind the line tie. These, like nearly everything else that goes to make up your spinning lure, are optional. The important thing to remember, though, is that weighted lure bodies shouldn't be placed ahead of the spinner blade, lest they interfere with its action.

Next select the smallest clevis that will work with the blade you select. French, Indiana, and willowleaf blades are commonly used with in-line spinners. Other varieties include the ripple, swing, and June bug. All but the June bug, which has a cut-out arm in its middle that fits over the shaft, require the use of a clevis. (June-bug spinners are often used for trolling and in combination with live bait, such as minnows.)

The size of the spinner blade you select should be determined by the size and weight of the lure body, and by the size of the hook you plan to use. For example, a relatively large No. 1 or No. 2 treble hook, such as you might select for largemouth bass or northern pike, would likely call for a quarter-ounce lure body, and this in turn would call for a No. 6 or No. 7 Indiana or French blade. Smaller lures, such as for panfish or trout, might also use a French blade, but more likely a willowleaf or swing blade. Lures smaller than one-quarter ounce generally call for the use of spinning tackle.

The lure body, either painted lead or natural or nickeled brass, usually goes on the shaft immediately behind the clevis that holds the blade. In June-bug construction, where weighted bodies often are not used, attractor beads can make up the entire lure body. Plastic tubing frequently is fitted over the shaft of the lure or the hook itself. Tubing used to separate the clevises in tandem-blade construction is also fairly common.

With line tie bent, spinnerbait components are added to the wire shaft in the order shown. Lure body, in this case, consists of the barrel of an old felt-tip pen and a bullet-shaped slip sinker.

The terminal loop or eye (the one that holds the hook) is usually of the open type, held closed by a coil-spring fastener after the hook is added. Alternatively, a closed loop can be used and the hook held on the lure by a split ring. If open-loop construction is selected, it follows that the coil-spring fastener must be the last thing added to the lure shaft before bending the terminal loop. An open loop is bent exactly as a closed or wrapped-end loop would be, except the wire is not twisted back around itself. Instead, a tag end about a quarter of an inch long is left after the terminal loop is bent, and the fastener is slipped up over this end to secure the loop after the hook is in place. Keep in mind that the length of shaft between the fastener and the terminal bend must be as long as the fastener itself, else it won't slip over the tag end of the wire. This is an efficient construction that allows hooks to be changed while fishing.

81

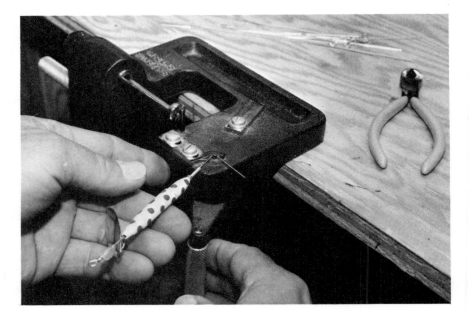

Components in place, author again uses Cabela's Spinner Maker to bend terminal loop.

Another way of making the terminal bend is to use a brass bead instead of a coil-spring fastener. Select a bead with an inside diameter large enough to accommodate two strands of the wire you are working with. Bend the end loop the same way as before, then slip the bead over both strands of wire. Now, with the spinner held in a vise, bend the tag end of the wire extending past the bead in a 90-degree angle and clip it off as close to the bead as possible. This results in a permanent loop, so the hook must be in place before it is bent. Alternatively, use a small split ring to attach the hook to the terminal loop.

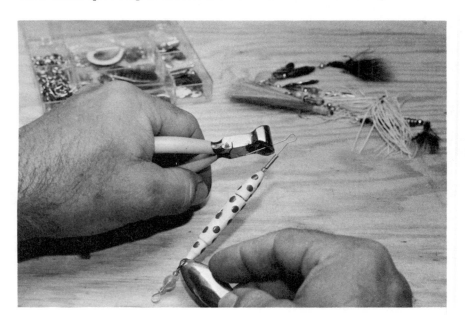

Spinnerbait shaft is clipped so that its tag end will fit under coil-spring fastener after hook is added. Open-loop construction allows hook to be changed easily without need for a split ring.

Treble hooks used with in-line spinners are often dressed with any one of the several materials—tinsel, hair, feathers, and such—used with jigs and spoons, and the procedure for tying is the same. Single hooks are used increasingly with in-line spinners, and these are often dressed with soft-bodied lures such as twister-tail worms, grubs, or minnows. The new "Keeper" hooks by Mister Twister, having a barbed shaft or "stinger" attached to the eye of the hook, are especially good for this purpose, as they keep the soft lure in line with the spinner shaft while allowing the point of the hook to be buried in the body of the lure. You may find that a swivel snap placed between the spinner and the line is required to prevent excessive line twist.

With the addition of a dressed treble hook and closure of terminal loop with coil-spring fastener, the in-line spinnerbait is ready to be fished. Other easy-to-make lures are shown in background.

In-line spinners, as previously noted, are easily made lures that allow your imagination to run free. Just about any cylindrical object can be incorporated in the body. I've used bullet- and egg-shaped sinkers painted in attractor colors, old springs that are tapered on both ends, even discarded felt-tip writing pen bodies.

In the latter construction, cut off the tip of the pen to a length of about two inches, push out the felt liner, and force an appropriately sized plastic bead into the cut-off end of the pen barrel. The bead should be glued in place with Duco cement. The tip end of the pen barrel is fitted onto the spinner shaft right behind the clevis, and a bullet-shaped slip sinker, blunt end first, is added for casting weight immediately behind the pen body.

It's difficult for me to imagine a well-stocked tackle box without a dozen or so in-line spinnerbaits. Equally difficult to imagine, however, are the prices these little bits of hair and hardware are selling for these days. The home craftsman can have the best of both worlds: For a modest investment in components and an even more modest investment in time and talent, he can fill his tackle box to overflowing with these versatile little lures.

8. Molding Plastic Worms and Other Soft Lures

I know for sure that soft-bodied lures have been in American tackle boxes since the turn of the century, and maybe a few years before. My grand-dad was a bass and trout angler of some repute, and his tackle box—which passed on to me upon his death in the 1930s—contained a number of molded-rubber crawdads, helgramites, crickets, and grubs. Most had been purchased in the early 1900s.

Like Mr. Ford's Model T of the same era, those turn-of-the-century rubber lures were available in any color you wanted—as long as it was black. My impression is that most of them were imported from Europe. Crude though they were by today's standards, they did catch fish. My grandfather used them regularly for Texas bass and often made trips to Colorado or New Mexico, where he used them with a fly rod at times when the rainbows were turned off to flies.

During the forties, what little natural rubber was available went into the war effort. But research to develop a synthetic rubber proved successfully and ultimately led to the plastic that is used to make soft-bodied lures today. All of the big worm manufacturers these days use a product known as liquid plastic or plastisol, and the same stuff—in two or three different formulations—is available to home hobbyists in quantities ranging from pints to five-gallon pails. In my experience, a quart, which sells for about six dollars, will make about 150 six-inch worms. This means that you can make your own worms for about a nickel apiece when the cost of coloring and other additives is figured in. Purchased in bulk through one of the catalog houses, these same worms will cost you nine to twelve cents each, and quite a bit more if you buy them at your local tackle shop. So the savings, though not monumental, make it worthwhile to mold your own worms and other soft lures if you fish with them as much as I do.

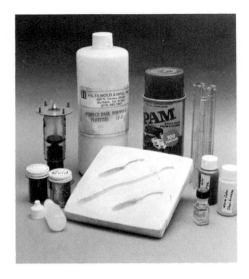

Equipment and supplies used for molding plastic worms include squeeze bottle for adding color, glitter flakes, purchased injector molds, plastisol, vegetable cooking spray, color concentrates, anise oil, and open molds of hard rubber or plaster, either purchased or homemade.

Making Your Own Molds

Our ol' friend plaster of Paris again comes into its own when we start making worm molds. The procedure is similar to, but just a little different from, the way we went about making jig molds. The main difference is that this time we'll be making and using single-piece open molds instead of the pinned types used in jig making.

For making worm molds, you'll need to use gallon-size milk cartons, which measure 5½ inches on the side and just under 8 inches on the diagonal. Assuming that you're planning to mold 6-inch or 7-inch worms, the 8-inch diagonal measurement of a one-gallon milk carton suits your purpose well. What I usually do is mold a large worm across the diagonal, and then stick in a couple of grubs or smaller critters in the corners to utilize fully the available space.

Prepare your milk carton by cutting it two inches from the bottom; then use a sharp knife to slit the bottom portion at each corner. Now use masking tape to hold the slit corners in position. Mix up your plaster to the consistency of light pancake batter and pour enough in the carton to fill it halfway up. (This means your mold will be one inch thick.) Let the plaster set up for a few minutes, then press into it whatever worm or soft-bodied lure you want to cast. The pattern lure should be lightly coated with Pam or a vegetable oil to keep it from sticking to the mold when removed. Press the pattern lure into the soft plaster until it is almost covered.

Cut milk carton, as described in text, and slit at corners.

86

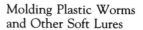

Molding Plastic Worms
and Other Soft Lures

Tape carton at corners, spray inside with cooking spray, and pour about an inch of plaster into the carton.

Spray pattern worms with cooking spray and press them into soft plaster to create molded cavities.

Should you want to make a mold for a soft lure you don't already have in your tackle box, you can carve a pattern from soft wood. After carving, sand well and coat with varnish or lacquer so that the surface is perfectly smooth. Again, coat lightly with Pam or vegetable oil before pressing the wooden pattern into the plaster. This approach gives good results, but it's obviously more time consuming.

After allowing the plaster to cure, remove the mold from the milk carton by peeling off the tape and opening the carton at all four corners. Now, before attempting to remove the pattern worm from the cavity it has created, use a straight edge or putty knife to scrape away enough of the plaster to expose the upper third of the worm. This will prevent the plaster from chipping at the edges of the cavity when the pattern worm is removed.

87

After plaster hardens, untape corners and open carton carefully to avoid chipping around edges.

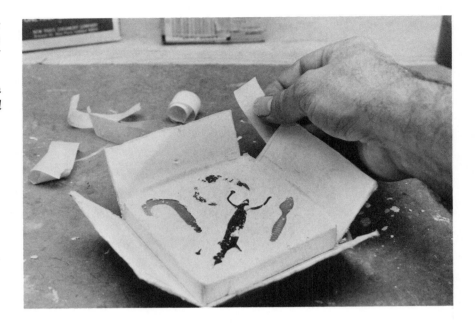

Beginning at the tail, gently remove the worm from the cavity. Use a rounded sucker stick, small dowel, or Dremel Moto-Tool to smooth the inner walls and bottom of the cavity. If you're molding a segmented worm, use a sharpened sucker stick to accentuate the ridges and depressions that will form the segments. With this done, place the mold in a warm oven (200 degrees Fahrenheit) for an hour or two to remove all the moisture. Leave the oven door open.

Use rounded sucker stick or Moto-Tool to smooth inner walls and bottoms of cavities; accentuate ridges and depressions that you want to retain in molded worms.

Plaster, by its nature, is porous, and, unless the mold is coated with a nonporous substance, will give an unwanted dull finish to your worms. After experimenting with several coating substances, including epoxy and fiberglass resin, I've found that the easiest and most effective coating to use is gloss Mod Podge. Not only does it give the perfectly smooth, nonporous surface needed, it also fills in any minor nicks or abrasions that may exist in the mold. Give the entire mold—surface and cavities—several coats of Mod Podge, and your worms will come out as slick and glossy as a wet Labrador.

Use gloss Mod Podge to paint cavities and impart glossy look to molded worms.

There are several excellent one-piece molds on the market, but by far the widest selection I've found is handled by Lure-Craft of Solsberry, Indiana. Lure-Craft molds are made from some sort of silicone-base rubber that's permanently bonded to a wooden frame. Their premium molds sell for just over nine dollars each, and they also offer an economy model (without the wood frame) that lists for about seven dollars. There's a fairly substantial discount for quantity orders. Almost incredibly, Lure-Craft makes over four hundred different molds for plastic lures. They also sell plastisol, coloring agent, scent, stoves, glitter—in fact, just about any and everything you can think of in the way of worm-molding equipment and supplies.

One problem with one-piece molds, albeit a minor one, is that the plastic bodies they produce are flat on one side, just like the manufactured worms were when they first came on the market about thirty years ago. The large worm manufacturers have overcome this problem by using big extruding machines costing several thousand dollars each. Home tackle makers, until very recently, had to content themselves with one-piece molds.

This situation has now been changed by a line of two-piece injection molds made by Hilts Molds of Burbank, California. These ingenious and relatively inexpensive little units are made to extremely close tolerances from a hard, clear plastic. After gaining a little experience in their use, I found that I could mold perfect baits every time.

The secret to these nifty little gadgets is a piston-type plunger that forcefully injects hot plastisol into the mold. You hold the mold in both

Purchased Molds

89

hands, push down on the plunger with your thumbs, and, presto, you have a perfectly formed round worm or grub. Hilts makes two different kinds of molds—one with a built-in reservoir and the other with an external reservoir-injector. I've found that the external-reservoir variety is quite a bit faster to use, because three molds can be filled or "shot" with a single filling of the plunger reservoir. The internal-reservoir model is held together with strategically placed thumb screws, and these take a little time to remove and replace each time a bait is molded.

My only objection to the external-reservoir molds is the plastic C-clamps provided with them. Like the thumbscrews, they take a bit of manual dexterity to remove and replace in a hurry. I solved this perceived problem by tossing away the C-clamps and replacing them with small spring clamps that not only go off and on a lot faster, but provide a good handhold when shooting plastic. A comprehensive set of instructions comes with each mold, including an admonition to spray the mold with a vegetable oil. The only problem I initially encountered was getting all the bubbles out of the plastisol when molding, but this was overcome with a little experience.

Several catalog houses carry the Hilts products. I got mine from Netcraft, which lists molds for $4.00 to $5.00 and the injector for $5.80. You'll need at least three molds if you expect to get any kind of production line going, but a single injector will serve. As yet, Hilts doesn't offer anywhere near the variety of configurations that Lure-Craft does. Netcraft, for example, lists only eight shapes—five worms and three grubs—in its current catalog. My prediction, though, is that more will be available shortly; the things are just too much fun not to go over big.

Working With Plastisol

Plastisol is a viscous, milk-colored liquid that turns crystal clear as you heat it. The recommended heating temperature is 325 degrees Fahrenheit, so an inexpensive electric hotplate is all that's required. Start by mixing the plastisol *well:* There are solids in the bottom that have to be thoroughly blended or your worms will be too soft and lack strength. Pour an inch or so of the plastisol into a small aluminum pan, place it on the burner, and stir it as it heats. It's possible to scorch it and ruin the batch if you let it get too hot.

Pour about an inch of plastisol into a small saucepan and heat it on a hot plate or similar heat source.

As you heat the plastic, you'll note the appearance of stringy lumps, but this is normal. As the heating process continues, the plastic will thicken, then lose its milky look, and begin to thin. If it begins to smoke, you've got your heat too high. When the now-syrupy liquid is clear and without lumps, it's ready to use. This is the time to add coloring agents to obtain whatever color you desire. I've yet to be convinced that it helps catch fish, but you can also add glitter at this point if you want. Eleven or twelve color concentrates are available, but all you really need are the basic colors—white, black, red, yellow, and blue. By experimenting with varying proportions of these basic dyes, you can get all the colors of a West Texas sunset. Equal portions of red and yellow, for example, will give orange; equal portions of red and black will give purple; one blue and three yellows will produce chartreuse. Not a whole lot of color concentrate is needed to produce most colors, depending of course on how opaque you want your worms to be. It's best to use an eyedropper to introduce the dye, stirring it into the plastic as you add a drop at a time.

Stir the plastic constantly as it heats; it will lose its milky look and become thin.

Color concentrate and glitter flakes (if desired) should be added to the plastic after it turns clear and thins.

I think it's a pretty general opinion in worm-fishing circles that black, purple, motor-oil, and blue worms produce best 90 percent of the time. Still, I like to have chartreuse and yellow worms in my box for early spring fishing when the water's still murky, and there was a day early last summer down in southern Illinois when I'd have killed for one more orange worm. For some unfathomable reason, that's all the big mamas were hitting that day, and my partner and I went through our meager supply long before it was time to come in off the lake.

How to Mold Worms

The basic operation of pouring plastic into one-piece (open) worm molds is about as hard as persuading the kid he ought to go fishing with you instead of mowing the lawn. There are some special effects—like two-color and harnessed worms—that we'll talk about in a few minutes, but right now let's get in there and root hog.

With your heated plastic (color added) about the consistency of hot-cake syrup, remove the pan from the burner and—beginning with the head—fill the cavity with a fine but steady stream that you can both see and control. You'll likely find it a little awkward at first to pour a steady, continuous stream, but after a surprisingly short time you'll have the hang of it. If you mess up the first few pours, no sweat: just pop the worms back into the heated plastic and stir 'em around until they're melted again. Use of a Hilts injector also simplifies pouring.

After adding color and glitter, pour liquid (hot) plastic into injector or, alternatively, directly into mold cavities.

If injector is used (a method advocated by the author), a small, steady stream of hot plastic is fed easily into the molds.

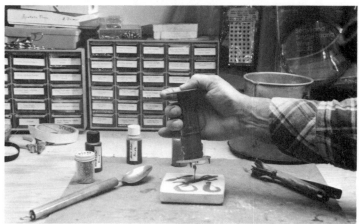

Plastic shrinks as it cools, so it's better to overfill the cavity slightly than to underfill it. Any overfill is easily trimmed off with scissors, razor blade, or X-acto knife and returned to the mix.

Your worms will be ready to remove from the mold in about two minutes. Rub your index finger gently over the worm just ahead of the tail until the tail pops free of the mold. Then, tail first, lift the entire body out of the mold. If you have trouble with them sticking, spray a *light* coating of Pam into the cavity. Have a few sheets of clean, lint-free paper or aluminum foil handy to lay the finished worms on. Don't pile them on top of each other; they can stick together while they're still warm. After you've poured a few dozen worms, or whatever your quota for the day is, trim the overfill from each of them and toss it back in the pan for future use. Ziploc sandwich bags work fine for long-term storage of excess plastic.

Allow about two minutes for the worms to "cure," then remove them from the mold tail first.

Spread molded worms and other soft-bodied lures on a sheet of aluminum foil until molding is done; then use X-acto knife to remove excess plastic.

With the molding operation completed, pour about half a teaspoon of vegetable oil (safflower oil works best because it's light and won't congeal) into a Ziploc bag and massage the bag until the oil is well distributed. Now put the worms—one color to the bag—into the oiled bag and knead it a little more until all the worms are lightly coated.

*Final step is to pour mixture of safflower oil
and anise concentrate into plastic bag, lightly
coating worms to remove human odor and
prevent sticking. Worms of different colors
should be stored separately.*

I buy natural (concentrated) anise oil at the drugstore and mix it into
the vegetable oil ahead of time. I don't count myself among those who
claim that scent is an attractor for predator fish like the black bass, but
I'll readily concede that human odor is a turn-off for any fish that swims.
Anise oil overpowers human scent, which can cling to soft-bodied lures
more readily than to hard lures, and on this basis I think its use is
worthwhile. Besides, I like the smell of licorice.

Some fishermen swear by worms done in two or more colors, notably
tails that are lighter than the bodies, as with the familiar "fire-tail" design. I've personally never found that different-color tails result in much
other than short strikes, but if your experience has been different, they're
faily easy to make. Reverse your order of pouring this time, and pour
the tail first. Then, with the plastic still hot, begin with a different color
and pour, head to tail, until the colors meld together. Hilts provides
instructions for making two-color worms with their injection molds. The
game plan here is to shoot the entire worm just as you normally would.
Then remove the worm from the mold, diagonally cut off whatever portion of the tail you want to replace with another color, return the worm
to the mold, and reshoot the worm with the second color. It works fairly
well, but it's a lot of bother.

Putting spots, stripes, bloodlines, and spider-web designs in worms
molded in one-piece (open) molds is also a fairly simple procedure. I've
used Hilts's injector for the purpose, but Lure-Craft sells a dispensing-
gun kit that works like a glue gun. You just replace the glue sticks with
sticks of premolded plastisol.

Use either the dispenser gun or the plunger injector to make spots or
a spider-web design in the bottom of the mold, pour in the plastic as
you normally would, then add additional spots or whatever to complete
the design on the top of the worm. To make bloodlines or internal spots,
pour the mold about half full, add the second (darker) color plastic with
dispenser gun or injector, then complete your pour to fill the mold. I've
had some difficulty getting all this done before the plastic hardens, and
I can see how working with a partner would really be helpful. Hilts's
dispenser gun, which melts the plastic as you dispense it, eliminates the
problem—but at a cost of nearly thirty dollars.

Nearly all the worm fishermen I know prefer to rig their worms Texas-style, meaning the point of the hook is buried in the body of the worm after being brought through the worm head and out again. A slip sinker, either bullet- or egg-shaped, is placed on the line before tying on the hook. The advantage of the Texas-style rig, and variations thereof, is that it makes a plastic worm about as weedless as any lure can be.

There are times, though—like when the fish are striking short or just mouthing the worm—when harnessed worms will catch more fish than a Texas-style rig. Sometimes called an Indiana rig, harness rigs call for two and sometimes three hooks held together by braided Dacron or monofilament line, and molded inside the worm body. Only the point and about half the bend of each hook is exposed; the shafts and eyes of the hooks, as well as the harness itself, are molded into the worm.

The scenario for making harness-rigged worms calls for the first hook (back from the worm's head) to be snelled. I don't know about you, but snelling hooks is pure torture for me: either my fingers are too big or my brain too small. To solve the problem, I use a handy (and cheap) little device known as Rudy's Snell Tyer (Rudy Masson Products, Burbank, California). It makes snelling almost easy.

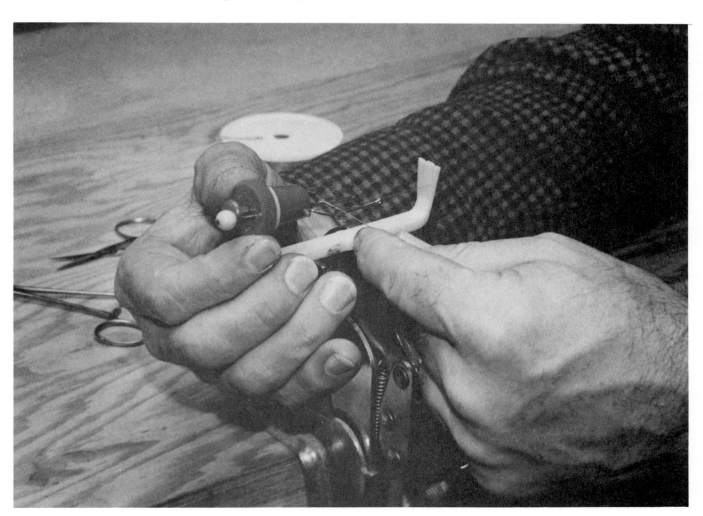

Snelling hooks, necessary in making harness-rigged worms, is greatly simplified by using a small devise called Rudy's Snell Tyer.

The eye of the front hook can be allowed to protrude from the nose of the worm, as with a Texas-rigged worm, or monoline can be extended from the worm's nose and a couple of beads and a propeller tied on. Either way, begin with a length of mono (or braided Dacron) about 16 inches long. Snell in the first hook about 8 inches from one end of the line, then tie on the second (tail) hook with a twice-through-the-eye clinch knot. The tail hook should be about 1½ or 2 inches from the worm tail in most designs, or at a point where you still have enough worm body to cover its shank.

If you're familiar with the snelled hooks you buy at the tackle shop, you know they have turned-down eyes. These don't work well with harnessed worms, because the eye wants to stick out through the worm body. My preference is for an Aberdeen hook, such as Eagle Claw's No. 202 or Mustad's No. 856, in size 1/0 or 2/0; much larger and you'll snag a lot, much smaller and you'll have trouble extracting the hook from the fish's mouth. You can use weedless hooks, of course, but I think they cause me to miss strikes when used with worms. (This is my Excuse No. 76.)

I usually make up a dozen or so worm harnesses and then melt my plastisol and start pouring. You can, if you don't mind a burned finger now and then, pour the entire work and then push the hooks and harness down into the still-soft plastic. I personally find it easier to fill the mold about a third of the way with plastic, place the hooks and mono in position, then pour the rest of the worm. The procedure is a lot easier if you work with a buddy and have him hold the hooks by their points with sharp-nosed pliers while you pour the plastic.

If you're making up rigs in which the eye of the front hook extends out the nose of the worm, merely trim back the nose to expose the eye after molding is complete. If you want to make rigs that include beads and a propeller forward of the worm, slip two plastic beads onto the monofilament line that extends from the worm nose after it's molded, followed by a small (No. 1) propeller, followed by another bead. Complete the rig by tying in a bowline knot that attaches to your fishing line.

Worms rigged with beads and propellers are sometimes powerful medicine for suspended bass and walleye. They're hard to cast because of their light weight, and you'll want to fish them with spinning tackle. Ninety percent of the time I fish Texas-rigged worms, but harness-rigged worms are worth having in your tackle box for special situations.

9. Making Wood and Plastic Plugs

The way some of my fellow scribes write about the ease with which the home craftsman can whip out a hand-carved lure sometimes leads me to wonder just how many they've actually carved themselves. Making a plug that looks good hanging on the wall (or used to illustrate an article) is no trick at all. Making one that catches fish is something else again.

The wood carving itself is not what requires time, patience, and more than a little inventiveness. Rather, the challenge comes in forming a tiny block of wood whose every action and movement somehow emulates that of a baitfish. The testing, tuning, and tinkering required to successfully duplicate an existing pattern, let alone come up with something better and different, is perhaps the ultimate challenge facing any tackle crafter.

When I started carving wooden plugs while still in college many years ago, there was ample reason for doing so. The plug patterns available thirty-five years ago were fairly limited, and the home craftsman had reason to expect he could build a better fish trap. I was fishing, in the late 1940s, a lure I made that closely resembled today's crankbaits. I've often wished I'd had the foresight (and the funds) to commercialize it. I suspect such stories are legend, hindsight being the relatively useless commodity that it is.

This chapter will tell you, as nearly as I'm able, how to carve plugs from wood and how to paint and finish—at considerable cost savings—plugs that are preformed of plastic. It's a pleasurable and satisfying pastime, one I hope you'll develop an interest in. But please, be forewarned that it's not as easy as some "experts" would have you believe.

Nearly everyone has his own favorite lure, depending a whole lot on how well it has performed for him over the years. But one man's perfume is another man's polecat, and the simple fact is that no single lure, or family of lures, will consistently catch fish under all conditions. There are just too darn many variables—time of year, light conditions, water temperature, and so on—that affect the feeding habits of the finicky adversaries we pit our wits against.

It hasn't always been so, but today's selection of wood and plastic plugs gives us fishermen a broader choice of retrieval speeds, action, color, size, and depth than just about any other family of lures. Depending on design and how we fish 'em, we can build or buy plugs that'll go deep or shallow, fast or slow, quiet or noisy, lazy or frenetic. Somewhere in every well-stocked tackle box is bound to be a plug that fits conditions and stands a good chance of turning on strikes, even on slow days.

That description obviously fits store-bought plugs as well as hand-crafted ones, and I've got more than a few of both in my tackle boxes. Aside from the self-realization (a four-bit word that means "fun") that comes from making your own plugs, the major attraction is cost. With many bass plugs fetching three to six dollars a copy these days, I figure that rollin' my own lets me put two or three lures in my box for every one I buy. That's a savings not too many fishermen can ignore, particularly those that fish the stickups of southern impoundments.

Plug Designs

If it weren't for the largemouth bass, I doubt there'd be a market for fishing plugs in the United States. Off the top of my head, I'd say that maybe 80 percent of all freshwater plugs being manufactured are sold to bass fishermen. The remainder are made or bought by muskie, walleye, and big-lake trout and salmon fishermen. Moreover, it's been that way as long as I, or anyone I've talked to, can remember.

Back in the twenties and thirties—and, in fact, until fairly recently—nearly all of the plugs in the tackle boxes of most bass fishermen were what, today, we call surface or top-water lures. It wasn't until some time in the sixties, as nearly as I can recall, that we began to really understand structure fishing and realize that largemouth bass don't spend most of their time in bays and backwaters. Surface lures were perfectly suited to the kind of spring and fall fishing most of us did.

Perhaps the earliest of the top-water lures was what most of us today would call a floater-diver. This is sort of a catchall term used to describe plugs that float at rest but make shallow dives when steadily retrieved. Most such lures being made today depend on a small plastic lip to pull them down, but the first floater-diver, whittled out of wood some seventy years ago by an Indiana fisherman, had an ingenious concave slot in the top of its head. Patented in 1916 by South Bend Tackle Company, it was named the Bass Oreno. I think it must have been out of print for several years, but it's being made again by Luhr Jensen. Another classic floater-diver, introduced by Heddon in 1920, is the Lucky 13, being made these days by Cotton Cordell.

Another fine old lure, which I guess you'd have to classify as a floater-diver even though it deserves a class all by itself, is the V-shaped Lazy Ike and its kissin' cousin the Flatfish. A similar design, Heddon's Tadpolly, is a favorite of Great Lakes trout and salmon fishermen, who use it in conjunction with downriggers.

Another classic plug design is the chugger. These lures have cup-shaped noses and tapered bodies that make them dart and gurgle on the surface when manipulated by the fisherman's rod. Chuggers have little action of their own, and everybody I know who fishes them regularly has developed a routine for making them perform. The chugger design that's been around the longest is Heddon's Chugger Spook, introduced in 1939. It was also, I believe, the first popular lure to be made of plastic.

Classic Lure Designs

Floater-Diver

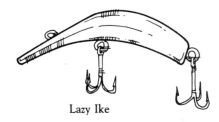

Lazy Ike

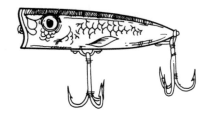

Chugger

Popper-type plugs, immortalized by Fred Arbogast's Hula Popper and Jitterbug, have been taking their share of bass and other fish for more than thirty-five years. These lures have exaggerated dish-shaped mouths or double-lobed metal lips that cause them to pop and gurgle like wounded baitfish or frogs. They have a built-in action of their own on steady retrieve, but work better for me when intermittently twitched (popped) and rested. Poppers make a lot of noise, and are great nighttime lures.

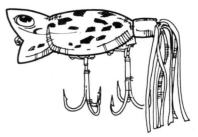

Popper (Hula Popper)

Stickbaits are torpedo-shaped lures that have no action at all of their own; their effectiveness depends on the fisherman's ability. Developed to a fine art by southern fishermen, particularly in Florida, the action imparted to stickbaits is popularly known as "walkin' th' dawg." A lot of stickbaits have been produced over the years, but the hands-down favorite for many years (since 1922) is Heddon's Zara Spook.

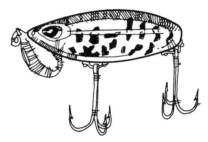

Popper (Jitterbug)

Spinner plugs have configurations similar to those of stickbaits, but with the important addition of propeller-shaped spinners fore and/or aft. The classic spinner plug was developed by Jack Smithwick (Smithwick Tackle Company), who thought it resembled a praying mantis and so named it the Devil's Horse. I'm not sure when the first Devil's Horse was sold commercially, but I do know my Uncle Willie Sweatmon fished it extensively down in East Texas and Louisiana during the thirties. I guess everyone has their own way of fishing spinner plugs, but the method that has proven most effective for me is a slow, steady retrieve punctuated by short, barely discernible twitches of the rod.

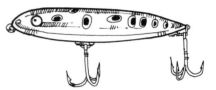

Stickbait

Minnow-type lures go by a variety of names and could be lumped in with the floater-diver classification of plugs. What we're talking about here, though, is the streamlined, baitfish lookalike invented in Finland by Lauri Rapala and imported into the United States by Normark Corporation since the late fifties. These amazing little lures, now being produced in a number of different sizes and colors, were first used by Finnish-Americans in the upper Midwest, where they proved just as effective for northern pike and walleye as they later did for southern bass.

Spinner Plug

Rapalas are made of balsa wood covered by a plastic-foil skin. A molded-in wire runs all the way around the body to form the hook eyes and line tie. The secret behind their inimitable action lies in their extreme buoyancy and a slightly concave Plexiglas lip that causes them to dive and dart erratically on retrieve. Dozens of other fake-minnow lures, made mostly of molded palstic, have been introduced over the years, and nearly all I've tried have worked well when I did my part.

Minnow-Type

Sinking plugs, which include the so-called countdown designs, haven't been around as long as the top-water lures, but plenty long enough to establish favorable reputations as fish-getters. Sinking plugs, which enable anglers to get down there where the fish live a good part of the time, derive their sinking ability from metal (usually lead) weights incorporated in their design. Countdown models, introduced by Rapala (Normark) about a dozen years ago, sink at a predictable rate of about a foot a second. The idea, of course, is that by counting slowly after your cast, you can determine the approximate depth of your lure. Sinking lures produce best for me when retrieved with a slow pumping action that allows them to alternately sink and rise.

Finally we come to the crankbaits, a lure design that has done for fishing in the late seventies and early eighties what Lauri Rapala's de-

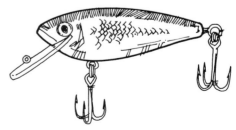

Crankbait

sign did in the early sixties. In short, they've darn near revolutionized bass fishing after a decade of plastic worms and spinnerbaits. When first I heard it used, "crankbait" was a sort of generic term used to describe any lure so designed that you could simply cast it out, crank it in, and depend on it to throb, wobble, dive, and otherwise comport itself in a manner practically guaranteed to trigger a strike.

When we talk about crankbaits today, most of us have in mind the large-lipped, rotund-bodied lures that dig deeply into the water on fast retrieve. Depending largely on the size of their lips and where their line ties are attached (on the lip or on the nose of the lure) crankbaits can be made to run deep, medium, or shallow.

It's obvious that deep runners must be large lures, because those big bodies are necessary to provide the extra buoyancy needed for a steep diving angle. The deep divers, designed to bounce off structure down to twelve feet or more, also have elongated diving lips, and line ties attached to their lips. The medium runners, intended to dive to depths of six to eight feet, have smaller lips, and the shallow runners have even smaller lips and line ties attached to their noses rather than their lips.

Most of the crankbaits in my tackle box are floater-divers, although some sinking and countdown models have proven popular. I prefer the floaters because they're a little easier to get back when they become hung up on underwater obstructions. And while it's true that these versatile lures will catch fish just castin' an' crankin', variable speeds and pumping action will nearly always prove more rewarding. Experimentation is the key to success.

Whether a crankbait that's been around only a few years, or a fine old plug that's been in production for half a century or more, every design mentioned will load up your stringer or livewell under the right conditions. If you're serious about catching fish (and you wouldn't be reading this book if you weren't), it's worth your while to have a selection of all of them in your tackle box. Doing so represents a sizable investment, and this alone can be valid justification for the dedicated fisherman trying his hand at making his own plugs.

What we're obviously doing is trading some of our free time for cash retained in our pockets, or devoted perhaps to upgrading our fishing boats or whatever. Even so, I question whether the endeavor is worthwhile unless we derive enjoyment from our own craftsmanship. The time involved in carving plugs, as compared, for example, with casting jigs or molding plastic worms, is substantial.

Selecting the Proper Materials

Commercial plugs are made today from a marvelous variety of materials, including several different types of hard plastic, compressed foam, and balsa and other light woods. For reasons of cost, all but a few of the larger manufacturers—notably Rapala and Bagley—have turned to molded plastic. I'm confident this has been a fortunate happening, for I doubt that the needs of 60 million fishermen could be met with wooden lures alone. Still, wood remains the traditional (and often preferred) material for commercial lure manufacture if the maker's reputation is such that he can recover his higher costs in the marketplace.

Lacking the massive machinery necessary to produce lures of molded plastic, the home craftsman is restricted to wood if he wants to create

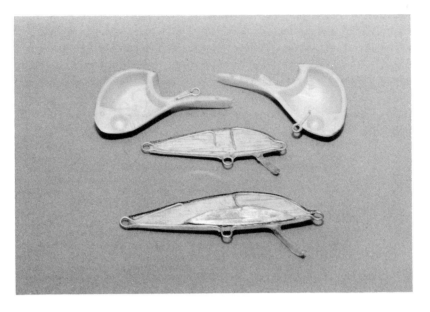

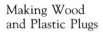

Commercially made plugs and their interiors. Top lure, of molded plastic, features a "rattle" chamber (round cavity at rear of lure) where a small ball bearing is seated. Center plug is one of Rapala's floating minnow-type models. Bottom lure is Rapala's "countdown" model. Note how wire is formed around the body of the two Rapalas to provide line ties and hook hangers, and how lower model has large lead inclusion to offset the natural buoyancy of the balsa wood, from which the lure is made.

his lures from scratch. A less time-consuming but (for me) a less satisfying alternative is to purchase unfinished plastic bodies that require only painting and hardware. Such bodies are available, in a variety of proven designs, from catalog houses such as Netcraft and Cabela's. The former, in particular, provides excellent patterns and instructions with its lure-making kit. Finishing preformed plastic bodies can result in cost savings of 300 to 400 percent as compared with purchasing name-brand lures.

A large selection of plastic (usually tenite) plugs are available as blanks for the home craftsman to finish. Sanding, painting, and the attachment of hooks and screw eyes are all that is necessary to create economical and serviceable lures.

Despite the wonders worked by Lauri Rapala, I don't consider balsa a good choice of wood for the hobbyist. While it's true that balsa has unequaled buoyancy, its softness requires an internal wiring system (rather than screw eyes) that's simply too tedious and uncertain for the home craftsman to become involved with. I've tried making lures from balsa on numerous occasions, and have yet to be satisfied with the results.

For many years, northern white cedar was *the* wood of choice for American-made fishing lures. There's still nothing better, but finding a reliable source for clear white cedar in the dimensions required for lure making has become extremely difficult. Fortunately, there are two woods readily available that are almost as good: basswood and white (sugar) pine. Both have the clear, straight grain that's essential to lure making, and both possess adequate buoyancy. Of the two, I think basswood has a slight edge because of its superior ability to retain screw eyes.

Because basswood is widely used for making furniture and children's toys (hobbyhorses and that sort of thing), it is stocked by most large lumberyards and can be easily ordered if not on hand. Even though many plugs can be made from 1-inch thicknesses, I prefer to buy 2-inch stock and rip it when necessary. For most of my lures, I start with 2-by-2-inch stock cut to appropriate length.

Working With Wood

With appropriately sized stock in hand, I begin by cutting out of heavy brown paper (a grocery bag works fine) a pattern that represents the top and side view of the lure I plan to make. If it's a design I expect to repeat several times, I trace the pattern onto thin (.050-inch) Plexiglas for permanence. Plexiglas, by the way, will also be used for diving lips, so buy a couple of half sheets from the lumberyard when you get your basswood. It's sold in varying thicknesses for storm-door material; I've found that the .050 and .10 thicknesses meet most of my requirements.

Wooden plug design begins at the desk, where a sketch of the proposed lure design is drawn on graph paper to proper dimensions.

Design is transferred from graph paper to heavy construction paper.

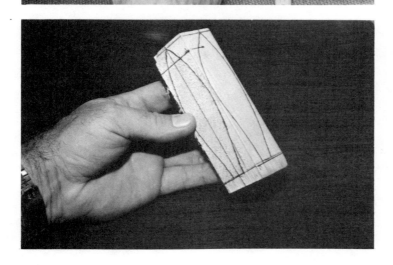

Paper cutout is transferred to a wooden block that has been sawed to appropriate dimensions.

Top, bottom, and side dimensions of the lure have been traced onto the wooden block, resulting in the patterns shown. Line drawn across nose of plug is where slot will be sawed for the diving lip of this crankbait.

With the pattern traced onto the wood you're working with, you are ready to begin the cutting (sawing or carving) operation. If the design you are making calls for a diving lip, saw the slot for it before you do anything else. Angles of 30 and 45 degrees will satisfy the requirements of most of the lures you'll make, so if you don't already have an adjustable miter box, make two small ones out of scrap lumber that just fit the wood blocks you'll be working with. Use a backsaw to cut the slot.

If the plug is to have a diving lip, sawing a diagonal slot for it in the wooden block is the first order of business. Miter box is handmade from three pieces of scrap hardwood.

103

With the lip-slot cut, take the wooden blank out of the miter box and start removing wood. I like whittling, so this is the way I remove 90 percent of my wood; the rest is taken off with a wood rasp and sandpaper in increasingly finer grades down to 320-grit. If you have a bench-mounted belt sander, it will greatly reduce the time you devote to wood removal.

Carving with a sharp pocketknife or one of the special knives made by X-acto quickly reduces the wood block to something that looks like a plug. Author's choice of wood is basswood.

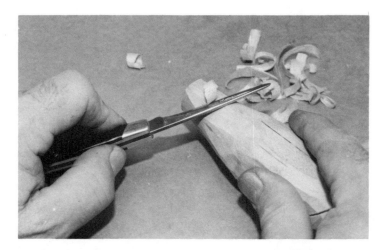

Power tools, such as this arbor-mounted drum/flapper sander, make the work go a lot faster.

Final sanding with progressively finer grades of sandpaper is done by hand.

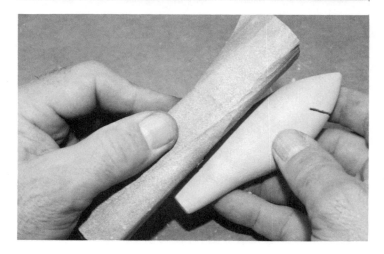

With the lure formed and rough-sanded, use a flat needle file and/or folded sandpaper to finish the lip-slot to precisely the dimensions required by the thickness of Plexiglas you are using. For minnow-type plugs, the .050-inch plastic works well; for larger lures, such as crankbaits, use the .10-inch materials.

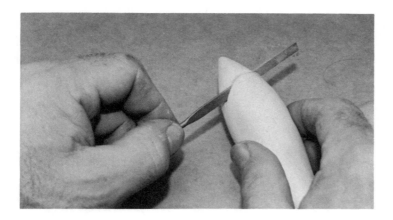

Diving-lip slot is smoothed and enlarged with a flat needle file.

As far as I've discovered, there isn't any really easy way to cut and form Plexiglas. Commercial users, such as storm-door installers, cut it with high-speed band saws, but my workshop is unfortunately bereft of such a device. So I cut a piece substantially larger than what I expect to wind up with using a hacksaw, and finish it to size on a sanding wheel. If you get it the least bit hot, the darn stuff curls up like a wilted rose, so the final finishing must be done with a fine file or a handheld sanding board. It takes a spell.

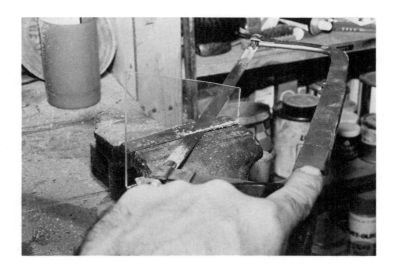

Plexiglas for diving lip is cut with a hacksaw and shaped with files and sandpaper. Power sanders can cause Plexiglas to melt.

Now we're ready to drill holes and insert screw eyes in them. Screw eyes come in a variety of sizes (2 through 20) and in both open and closed configurations. Size 4 is about the smallest I've ever found useful in making plugs, and size 8 about the largest. You obviously want to

105

use larger eyes for big lures with big hooks, and small eyes for small lures and hooks. A closed eye is always used for the line tie and also for affixing the hooks if you use split rings. In smaller lures, it's best to affix hooks directly to the eye, in which case you want to select an open eye, which is squeezed shut with sharp-nose pliers after the hook is in place. Screw eyes are cheap, and my suggestion is that you order sizes 2 through 10 in both closed and open design. This way, you'll always have a size that complements the lure you're assembling. It's not possible for me to be real precise about the right size of screw eye for a given lure, but in general, select the smallest eye that will accommodate, without crowding, the hook or split ring you plan to hang from it.

Crankbait, ready for assembly and painting, consists of body, two treble hooks, two split rings, three screw eyes, and Plexiglas diving lip.

With screw eyes selected, mark the positions where they will go on the lure and drill the tiniest holes that will accommodate them. Remember, you want the threads to bite into the wood real good.

We'd best talk right here about proper hook positioning. The location of the tail (terminal) hook and the line tie are obvious, but the right location for the belly hook takes a little more thought. Personally, I never *ever* put more than two treble hooks on a lure, and in fact remove the forward belly hook from lures I buy that have three of them. I figure two treble hooks—that's six points—are enough to catch any fish, and I don't want to have to worry about another when I'm getting a big ol' bass or northern out of my net.

Okay, where to hang the hooks? On crankbaits, the belly hook properly belongs right at the deepest part of the belly; on small stickbaits and minnow-type lures it should go a third of the way back from the nose; and on larger (fatter) lures it belongs just a tad farther back toward the tail. If your lure doesn't run like you think it should with this arrangement, try larger or smaller hooks. We'll come back to tuning and testing your lures in just a little while.

Now, with holes drilled for the screw eyes, give your lure body its final sanding with 320 or finer sandpaper. Coat the threads of the screw eyes with Duco cement and screw them into place. At this time, if you're working with a design that calls for it, you should also cement the diving lip into place.

Screw eyes are inserted into the plug body
after their threads have been coated with Duco
cement.

Diving lip is cemented in place as final stage
of assembly before sealer coat and paint.

I think you'll find, as I have, that your greatest success will be in
carving top-water plugs. The photographs on pages 102–106 show how
to make a large crankbait, which I selected simply because it's one of
the more difficult to make. If you master it, simpler lures like stickbaits,
chuggers, and spinner plugs should prove a snap.

One problem you'll have with deep-bodied lures like crankbaits is their
propensity to float on their side. To overcome this, you'll need to drill
a hole about three-eighths of an inch in diameter and maybe half an
inch deep in the bottom of the plug between the diving lip and the
belly hook. Into the hole, pack and glue as many flattened lead BBs as
necessary to make the lure float in its proper upright position. What
you want is just enough weight—lead plus hooks and other hardware—
to make the plug float half-submerged when at rest. This must be done,
of course, prior to painting, and some experimentation will be required.

Just this past summer, I experimented with creating neutral-buoyancy
plugs, again by implanting lead weights in their bellies. If you're not
familiar with the term "neutral buoyancy," let me explain. It simply means
that the lure neither goes up nor down in the water by itself, but remains at whatever level its diving lip takes it on retrieve. You've got
neutral buoyancy when you put your lure in the water and it submerges
to where its top barely breaks the water line. Lure makers are just be-

107

ginning to introduce these plugs, but I believe you'll be hearing more about them as fishermen discover how effective they are on suspended fish.

The Essential Sealer Coat

This will be a brief section, but I consider it so essential to producing long-lasting wooden plugs that I want to highlight it.

Anyone who's been around long enough to remember the wooden plugs of thirty or forty years ago will recall how, after a few seasons of use, the paint began to chip and crack and the screw eyes rusted out. This occurred because plug makers of that era didn't have the modern epoxy plastics or laminates with which to undercoat their wooden bodies before applying paint. Such is no longer the case: today, all manufacturers use plastic in some form or another, and it pays the home craftsman to do likewise.

Over the years, I've tried just about every wood sealer on the market, and while some are better than others, I've never found one that was totally satisfactory. The best product I've found for keeping water in the lake where it belongs is an epoxy laminate made by Behr Process Corp. called Build 50. This two-part epoxy is the same stuff they use to make those superslick bars and tabletops. There may be other two-part epoxies that will do the trick as well, but once I've got a winning horse I don't like to switch jockeys.

The author prefers to use a sealer coat of two-part epoxy, such as Behr's Build 50. Most epoxies require careful measurement of resin and hardener.

Just mix up the epoxy and brush it on; the directions are on the can. Be sure you get plenty around the base of the hook hangers and line tie and where the diving lip (if you're using one) enters the wood. Get all the bubbles out by blowing on them or puncturing them with a straight pin, then hang the lure by its line tie for five to seven hours until the epoxy has cured. Now we're ready to paint our lures in patterns and colors that will trigger strikes.

*Epoxy sealer is brushed on after screw eyes
and diving lip are in place. Care should be
taken to seal holes created by eyes and lip.*

Effective Colors
and Patterns

Until lure manufacturers introduced the so-called "naturalized" or photo-finish patterns that seek to imitate perfectly the appearance of baitfish, the colors and patterns used to make fish strike remained pretty much the same for many years.

I personally think the jury is still out on the relative effectivness of naturalized patterns, but extensive research by marine biologists has revealed some pretty amazing things about colors that attract and repel fish. In controlled tests, the scientists found that while bass can be provoked (tempted?) into striking a lure of almost any color, they have a decided preference for blues and greens. Similarly, unless they are in an extremely aggressive mood (as when spawning), bass are repelled by yellow and gold colors. Not only do these findings fly in the face of what a lot of us have believed for a lot of years, they argue against the effectiveness of naturalized lures.

The attractiveness of blues and greens, especially in our deeper lakes and impoundments, is easily explained by the fact that colors in these wavelengths are known (through oceanographic experiments) to refract light at greater depths than any other color. Red, for example, becomes jet black at depths of fifty to sixty feet; orange becomes black, and yellow becomes white. The only colors that persist, remaining essentially unchanged, under low-light conditions are those in the blue-green spectrum.

As for the fish-repelling qualities of yellow and gold, I have my doubts. I recall having fished Toledo Bend reservoir down in East Texas one spring a few years ago when minnow-type lures with gold finishes were outfishing anything else in my box by a wide margin. Also, I remain convinced that yellow is the most effective color for eyes.

Many other facts that scientists have reported about bass and other fish simply confirm what we've known for years. For example, they're more nearsighted than Aunt Tilly and prefer areas of subdued light. These factors should also influence the way we finish our plugs. Virtually all

109

baitfish have white or light-colored bellies, and since fish most often see the underside of lures first, it follows that the undersides should be painted white. At the same time, we need to create a silhouette appearance that old Mr. Myopic can see, and this suggests that darker colors are more effective for surface lures fished under low-light conditions.

It's now been established that bass's eyes, like ours, have both rods and cones, which means that they *can* distinguish colors. This brings us around to the fluorescent colors that have become popular in recent years. Tests have shown that fluorescent yellows, oranges, and reds retain their true surface colors at much greater depths than do their nonfluorescent counterparts, but I'm not sure this is an advantage. I was fishing the gin-clear waters of Texas's Blanco River a couple of summers back and watched as a small bass charged my fluorescent lure with mayhem obviously in mind. Then, about two feet from the lure, he put on the brakes and darted the other way. Perhaps the fluorescents allow fish to see our artful imitations a little *too* well. Since that experience, I've continued to use fluorescent lures, but only when water turbidity is high.

Although I remain firm in my belief that, under most conditions, sound and action are more important fish attractors than color, I've had too many experiences suggesting the importance of color to discredit it. There have been times when lures identical in every respect except color did not produce equally. In common with most fishermen, I read all the literature, try to digest all the scientific findings—and continue to load my tackle box with a variety of designs and a rainbow of colors. Somewhere in there, I know I've got just the right combination.

How to Paint and Pattern

As discussed in the chapter on jig making, any number of excellent lacquers and enamels are available. Nearly anything that works okay on lead heads will, in my experience, work equally well on plugs. It's not a good idea, however, to combine lacquers and enamels on the same plug, as one will sometimes cause the other to blister. When lighter or fluorescent colors are being used, a white primer coat will embellish their appearance. Generally speaking, I have better results when applying the lightest colors first, then adding various gradients through the darkest color that will be used on a given lure.

A variety of paints, enamels, and lacquers in both spray and brush-on formulations are available to the lure maker. In painting plugs and other lures, care must be taken not to use finishes that are incompatible, else peeling and blistering will occur.

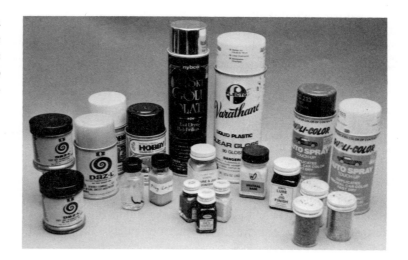

As a practical matter, most of my plug finishing involves a combination of brush and spray painting. I prefer to spray on the basic colors—as, for example, a white belly and silver sides—then add details such as eyes, gills, and back stripes by hand. The gradation from one color to another isn't marked on most baitfish, and I find that I can achieve gradual color changes more readily by spraying than with a brush.

A great help in spraying patterns—as, for example, the typical black-and-orange perch pattern—is a vinyl masking material sold by Netcraft, among others. The vinyl comes in small (4-by-6-inch) sheets, which you mark and cut to pattern, peel off its backing, and then smooth into place on the lure body. It conforms to the irregular contours of a plug better than anything else I've found and can be removed without peeling underlying paint.

An excellent minnow-scale pattern can be achieved by using another product, called scale netting, that's also available from Netcraft. It's taped tightly into place over the back and down the sides of the lure body, then lightly spray-painted over an underlying paint of a contrasting color. Typical color combinations are black over silver, silver over black, or dark blue over a lighter blue or silver. It gives a very appealing appearance that closely resembles the scales of a small shad or minnow.

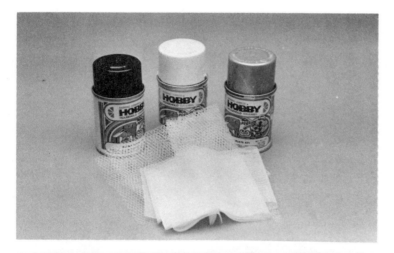

Scale netting, sold in two pattern sizes, is used in combination with spray paint to create realistic minnow-scale patterns on plugs.

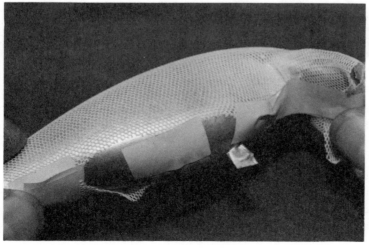

In use, scale netting is taped to a lure body that has been painted in an underlying contrasting color.

Scale netting in place, the plug body is hung in a painting box and spray painted.

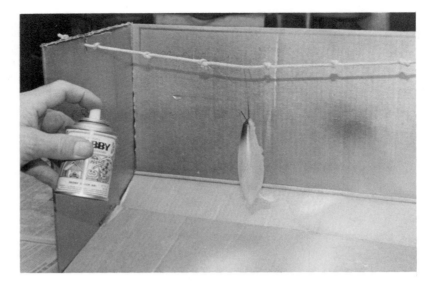

The eyes of the lure are best added after all other painting has been completed by using the heads of finishing nails. Typically, a large nail is used to make the yellow iris of the eye, then (when this paint is dry) a smaller nail is used to make the black pupil. Alternatively, the rounded tip of a small dowel can be used to make the iris. For larger dots, a small squeeze bottle (like those that eyedrops come in) can be used to good effect.

Spotting in eyes with the heads of finishing nails is one of the final touches in painting the lure.

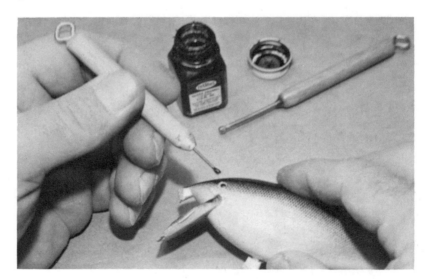

A mottled-frog finish can be achieved by using a square-tipped brush to dapple on orange or yellow spots over a dark green finish or, alternatively, black or brown mottles over a light green background. Remember, though, that even frogs have off-white, yellowish bellies.

Crawdad patterns, which have proved effective for me in lakes where these small crustacea are a natural food, should have orange bellies and brown uppers, highlighted with random black lines. Despite the fact that crawfish are bottom dwellers, surface plugs painted in crawdad pattern and fished in shallow water in early spring have produced well for me.

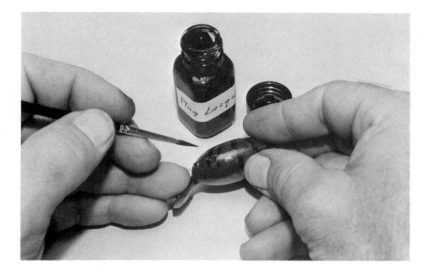

Crawdad patterns have proved to be effective fish getters for years. Colors are orange bellies and brown uppers, highlighted by random black lines.

My theory of lure design is that we are endeavoring only to create an illusion that will, for a brief instant, provoke an aggressive action by a predatory fish. For this reason, I keep my designs fairly simple. Still, such niceties as red gill stripes, random black spots over silver sides, and random lines (such as in the crawdad pattern) add attractiveness—and presumably fish-getting ability—to most lures. If not overdone, glitter adds to the light-refracting capability of a lure. To apply glitter, spray the painted body with lacquer and sprinkle the glitter on *lightly*.

If not overdone, glitter flakes add to the light-refracting ability of a lure.

A simple but effective trick for adding black back stripes, in particular, is to use a permanent felt-tip marker, the kind used for marking laundry. If your hand's not too steady, this method is easier than painting in stripes by hand. In my experience, colors other than black do not adhere well to plugs.

113

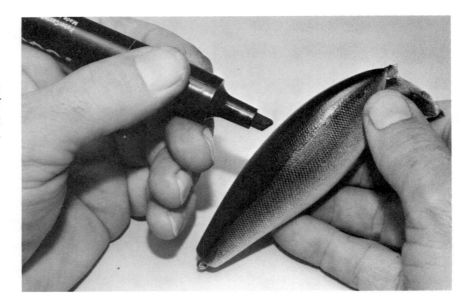

Following scale painting, permanent felt-tip marker is an easy and convenient means of applying the black back stripe. Lure body must be sprayed with clear plastic or lacquer after marking pen is used.

After finish painting has been completed, and especially if glitter or felt-tip marker has been used, I highly recommend a coat or two of clear lacquer or, better still, a clear gloss plastic finish such as Verathane, sprayed over the entire body of the plug. The diving lip should, of course, be masked if Plexiglas has been used.

Testing and Tuning Your Plugs

The story goes that back about 1936, when Lauri Rapala began carving his original balsa minnows, he tank-tested and hand-tuned every lure he made. It's a good story, and one I believe because I want to. Today, I believe that every Rapala, or any other factory-made lure, is individually tested about the way I believe ol' Lem Motlow sips every fifth of Jack Daniel's that comes off the bottling line.

Truth to tell, modern replicating machines have made such time-consuming chores unnecessary, but home craftsmen face a little different situation. We're not turning out thousands of lures every week, and we're not paid by the hour. Testing and tuning every lure we make is not only essential, it's fun.

My plug-making buddies down in Texas find their backyard swimming pool handy for this sort of thing. Private pools ain't the norm in the Chicago suburbs where I now live, and those that do exist are drained five months out of the year. But if you, like me, find yourself shy a backyard pool and unable to get out on the lake every weekend, there's still a lot you can do to make sure your creation works as it should.

Before you ever apply the first coat of sealer or paint, fit your plug out with the hardware (screw eyes, hooks, diving lip, and such) you expect it to wear, and put it in a tub or bucket filled with water. Note how it rides in the water. Does it sit level in the water or, if a diver, with its head slightly lower than the tail? Does it show any inclination to flop over on its side? Have you positioned your hooks and line tie in the proper places?

Left over from a long-ago time when the kids grew guppies, I have a fair-size fish tank that I find ideal for testing lures. With it, I'm able to observe both the way the plug rides in the water and how it looks from a fish-eye view. If it doesn't look right to me, I begin by replacing the hooks with ones that are a size smaller or larger. If this doesn't seem to help, I try moving the position of the belly hook back or forward. On occasion, some additional sanding is required to reshape the body fore or aft.

Despite my wife's snide remarks about "Jim's playing with his rubber duckies again," I manage to get to the root of basic design problems while sitting on the edge of the bathtub. For this final test, I use the forward section of an ultralight rod fitted with a couple of feet of light mono to swim the lure back and forth in the tub. It's not the perfect solution, but it gives me an idea of how the lure will run out on the lake.

In common with fitting guides on a rod blank, carving lures that catch fish is largely a matter of trial and error. For obvious reasons, as much of your testing and tuning as possible should be done and problems corrected before the lure is painted. After painting, I give my plug the ol' bathtub test one more time. If it runs true and, to the limited extent possible, looks like it has the kind of action I'm looking for, I have no qualms about making up several more of the same design. If, on the other hand, it fails the test, I don't mind throwing it in the scrap box.

The only true test of any lure—store-bought or homemade—comes when you're back in the boat and out on the lake. Does it cast well? If it's a stickbait, will it "walk" like it should? If it's a crankbait or floater-diver, does it dig in like it's supposed to on retrieve? And finally, after fair trial, will it catch fish?

Final tuning should be done while you're out on the lake. If your lure runs to the right or left, use sharp-nose pliers to bend the line tie slightly in the direction the lure tends to run. If, perchance, you've structured the lip of a diver of aluminum rather than the more prevalent Plexiglas, a slight downward bend will cause your lure to run deeper. Also, lighter line will cause plugs to run deeper; if you are casting with a level-wind rig and relatively heavy line, switch to a spinning outfit and light line.

It's painfully true that not every plug-making effort is rewarded with success, any more than we always return home with full stringers. Making plugs requires an adventurous spirit and a willingness to experiment. But then, come to think of it, isn't that what fishing is all about?

10. Making Spoons

Nobody knows who made and used the first spoon, but it's a pretty safe bet that it has been used to catch fish longer than any other artificial lure. Not only is it likely the most ancient of lures, it is also the most universally used. It has been cast, trolled, and jigged to catch virtually every fish that swims—from bluegills to barracuda—in both fresh and salt water. I doubt there's a tackle box in the nation that doesn't contain at least a few.

Strange to say, despite their ancient vintage and universal appeal, the spoons we use today—that is, those formed to provide fish-getting action as well as light refraction—are fairly recent innovations. Until 1912, when Lou Eppinger introduced the antecedent of his now-famous Dardevle, spoons used by fishermen had about as much built-in action as the one used at deer camp to stir mulligan stew. For at least three-quarters of a century before Mr. Eppinger's invention, the old Buell spoon or variations thereof was what everyone used. They had flutes and scallops and hammered finishes, but for all intents and purposes they looked like soup spoons with the handles removed.

Lou Eppinger changed that by hammering from a brass blank a spoon that was shaped like a teardrop and had subtle convolutions that made it wiggle and wobble. Just as most of the spoons used prior to 1912 were variations of the Buell design, many of them today are variations of the Dardevle design. It's hard to improve on perfection.

Tools and supplies used in making spoons include (from left) hair or other material for dressing hooks, sheet brass, treble hooks and split rings, ball peen hammer, wood-carving knives, wooden anvil for forming spoons, and auto-body spray paint.

117

The Forming Operation

Unlike my approach to spinnerbaits and plugs, wherein I continually experiment with my own designs and patterns, I'm pretty well convinced that spoon design has evolved about as far as it's likely to go. Hence, the spoons I make from hammered brass blanks are blatant imitations of originals manufactured by others. I doubt they'll ever replace all the Dardevles, Krocodiles, and Silver Minnows in my tackle box, but spoons are fun and inexpensive to make.

I begin with two "sacrificial" spoons of identical size and design taken from my tackle box. One of these is hammered flat to provide a pattern for tracing. The other is left in its original configuration to assist in hollowing out the wooden form (anvil) that will be used in shaping the copies.

Flattened sacrificial spoon is used to trace outline on hardwood block where forming anvil will be burned and carved out.

To make an anvil, select a piece of 1-by-2-inch hardwood (I get all I need by scrounging grocery-store alleys for packing crates) and cut it to a convenient length of about ten inches. Using the flattened pattern spoon, trace an outline on the wooden block. Adjust your propane torch to a fine flame and burn out wood within the confines of the outline. Now use a small concave wood-carving knife or Dremel Moto-Tool to remove the burned wood. Repeat this procedure until a spoon-shaped hollow begins to emerge.

Wood is burned out with propane torch to simplify the task of creating a forming cavity or anvil.

Concave wood-carving tool is used to remove burned wood, followed by sanding until a smooth cavity is created.

At this point, take the second sacrificial pattern spoon and heat it glowing hot with your torch. Press this pattern spoon firmly into the hollowed-out anvil to burn out additional wood. As you progress, alternatively burning and removing wood, the anvil will begin to take on every detail of the pattern spoon. In the final stages, apply your torch directly to the spoon as it lies cradled in the anvil cavity.

Use sandpaper to smooth the wood pattern you've created until it conforms perfectly to the original spoon. Assuming you work at about the same speed that I do, we're talking about a time investment of perhaps an hour from beginning to end. Now we're ready to begin our metal work.

Any sheet brass in thicknesses of .030 to .050 inch will work fine for our purpose. Because of a long-standing relationship (knife making is another of my hobbies), I obtain my sheet brass in convenient 4-by-8-inch sizes from Atlanta Cutlery Company of Conyers, Georgia. It's not, however, a difficult commodity to come by, and you can likely find other sources by calling around town.

Lay your *flattened* pattern spoon on the brass and scribe around its outside diameter. Also, because the location of holes for hook and line tie are critical, mark and center-punch these at this time. It's also a good idea to drill the holes, using a ⅛-inch bit, before you begin cutting out the brass blank. I use aviation snips for my brass cutting, but if you don't feel like investing in these rather expensive tools (a set of three is required for right-hand, left-hand, and straight cuts), a hacksaw will do the job just about as well.

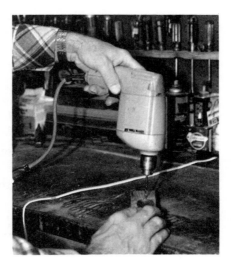

Before forming spoon, mark and drill holes for hook and line tie.

Cut the blank to within about 1/16 inch of the line you've scribed, then use a file or fine-grit grinding wheel to finish the blank to exact dimensions. Finish the edges of the blank well; it's a lot easier to do it now than after your spoon is formed. Also, use 400-grit sandpaper both to finish the edges and to remove any scratches on the surfaces of the blank. If you have a buffing wheel or a bench grinder, use it to put a perfect finish on the spoon blank.

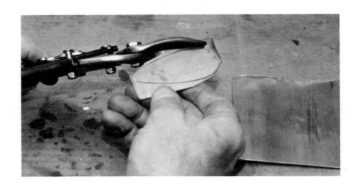

After scribing line using sacrificial spoon as pattern, cut out spoon blank with aviation snips or hacksaw.

Finish spoon blank with bench grinder and/or flat file.

At this point, you need to make a decision as to whether you want to put a hammered or smooth finish on your spoon. If it's the former you want, use the peening face of an eight-ounce mechanic's (ball peen) hammer to shape the blank. If you want a smooth finish, you must use a rubber-tipped hammer. Sears sells an excellent hammer with hard rubber on one face and nylon on the other for about $13.00. They also sell replacement rubber tips for $1.49. I bought one of these and then ground down the peen on an old mechanic's hammer so the rubber tip would fit over it. As they come from Sears, the rubber tips have square faces, and these also should be ground down to a rounded or convex configuration.

Using whichever hammer you select (depending on desired finish), place the brass blank in your wooden form and peen it with repeated light blows. The center portion of the blank will quickly conform to the contour of the anvil, but the edges of the spoon will remain wavy for a time. Don't worry. Just keep peening away and the entire spoon eventually will take on the precise shape of the form. It's not nearly as difficult a job as I imagined it would be before I tried it.

Form spoon blank by peening it while held in wooden anvil. After repeated light blows, the spoon will take on the precise configuration of the anvil cavity.

Your spoon will have taken on a rather dingy appearance from peening, but this quickly disappears with a good metal polish and some judicious use of elbow grease. We're nearly home.

Dressing and Hardware

It's sort of ridiculous to speak of hardware on a lure that's all hardware, but what we have to consider here is how to hang and dress the gizmo that catches the fish—the hook. We can use treble or single hooks, dress them with Fishair or other material, and even incorporate stainless-steel leader wire to make them weedless. I use spoons more frequently for pike than for bass and lean to the superior penetrating and holding ability of trebles. If this is your choice, I recommend dressing them by tying in natural or synthetic hair. The procedure is essentially the same as for dressing jigs, except of course you have two more hook points to work around. Begin by wrapping the hook shank from a point just below the eye to a point just above where the shank separates into three parts. Now wrap in small bits of hair, about six of them, so that the shank is completely covered and the points disguised. For pike-sized spoons, I like for the hair to extend an inch or so beyond the hook. After all bits of hair are in place, give the entire shank a couple more wraps and tie off with half-hitches. As with jigs, the entire wrapped portion is coated with head cement and painted.

Pike and other toothy fish chew up hair dressings pretty fast, and if you don't plan on replacing them every few seasons, a somewhat less effective but frequently used approach is to cover the shank of the hook with plastic attractor tubing. These can be bought, or stripped from large-gauge electric wiring. If you live in an area where home building is going on, you can quickly pick up enough scrap wiring to last you several years.

Split rings are used on both ends of spoons, both as line ties and hook hangers. Ring sizes should conform to the size of the spoon and its hooks, with size-4 and -5 rings being about right for most applications. It's easiest if you put the rings on the spoon first, then add the hooks.

Single and double hooks, as well as trebles, should be considered for use with spoons. Both are somewhat more snag-free than trebles and often to be preferred for trolling. For trolling, I prefer using a narrow, elongated spoon such as the Mepps Syclops or Luhr Jensen's Krocodile. Although somewhat heavier brass (about .060 inch in thickness) is required to make these spoons, they are well within the capabilities

121

Making Spoons Weedless

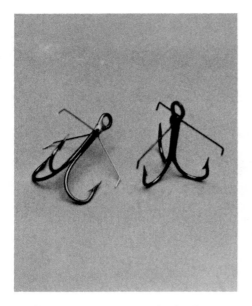

Treble hooks on spoons and other lures are easily made weedless by soldering fine stainless-steel wire on their shanks.

Making "Silver Minnow"-Type Spoons

Components necessary to make a weedless Silver Minnow–type spoon include (from left) stainless-steel wire bent to form weed guard, "pop" rivet, drilled and slotted brass blank, hook with large or open eye, and split ring.

of the home craftsman. I frequently hang double hooks on spoons such as these when used for trolling, and sometimes single hooks dressed with plastic grubs when going after bass.

One of the problems inherent in spoons, especially those hung with treble hooks, is their propensity to snag on every underwater obstacle that comes along. Trebles can be made weedless, if not totally snagless, by soldering fine stainless-steel leader wire (about .015-inch diameter) to their shanks just below the eye. The procedure isn't difficult.

To begin, cut two pieces of leader wire about five inches long and twist them together five or six times at their centers. What you have now is essentially a cross or X. Snip off one of the legs of the cross so that only three legs remain. Bend the wire so that you form a Y. Now, using your round-nose pliers, bend the twisted section of the wires into a U-shaped curve. Fit the U through the eye of the hook so that one leg of the weed guard is positioned over each point of the hook.

Clamp the hook in a small vise (or vise-grip pliers) and "tin" the eye and upper shank of the hook by applying a small amount of solder. Also tin the twisted portion of the weed guard. Use flux or an acid-core solder for best results. Now, with the weed guard held in position with forceps or hackle pliers, apply a drop of solder to the twisted portion of the weed guard immediately below the eye of the hook. Give the solder a moment to harden, then bend the tip of each leg of the weed guard about ⅛ inch from its end. The legs of the weed guard should project out just a little past the hook points, but far enough from them so that hooking ability isn't compromised. Hang the hook on your spoon with a split ring, and you've created a spoon as weedless as you can make it without also making it fishless.

One of my favorite bassing lures consists of a Johnson's Silver Minnow spoon dressed with a long strip of pork rind. If you're not familiar with the Silver Minnow pattern, what it is is a spoon with a single hook soldered or riveted to its underside and fitted with a Y-shaped wire to make it weedless. I've found that making these isn't much more difficult than making a standard-type spoon, and I'd like to tell you how to go about it.

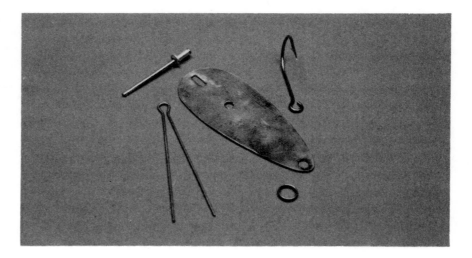

Begin just as you would in making a regular spoon, with these two exceptions: While the brass blank is still in its flat stage (before forming), cut a slot (instead of a round hole) in the large end of the spoon. This is done by drilling two or three parallel holes with a $\frac{5}{64}$-inch bit, then squaring off the slot with a flat needle (jeweler's) file. The finished slot should be about $\frac{1}{4}$ inch long and just slightly wider than the shank of the hook you'll be using.

Pass the point of the hook through the slot and mark, on the brass blank, the place where the eye of the hook is to be located. Using a $\frac{1}{8}$-inch bit, drill a hole at this point, making sure that it is in line with the slot and line-tie hole you've already made. Now form and finish the spoon as previously described.

We're going to use a hand or "pop" riveter to fix the hook and weed guard to the spoon, and the smallest pop rivet I've found is $\frac{1}{8}$ inch. This means that the hook we use must have an eye that's at least as large as the diameter of the smallest rivet. Trailer hooks have eyes that are big enough, but they're fairly expensive. I've found that size 2/0 salmon hooks by Mustad work well. They're exceptionally strong and have open eyes plenty big enough to accommodate a $\frac{1}{8}$-inch rivet.

Your next step is to cut a 5-inch length of stainless-steel leader wire of .018- to .020-inch diameter. Bend the wire in the middle to form an eye, just as you would when making an in-line spinnerbait. Holding the eye you've made with pliers, put a bend of about thirty degrees in each leg of the weed guard. Now, with the legs pointing out from the spoon, place the eye of the weed guard *under* the eye of the hook and rivet both hook and weed guard in place. The flange of the rivet, along with the weed guard and hook, goes on the under (concave) side of the spoon.

After forming and assembling as described in text, hook and weed guard are riveted in place.

With the rivet in place, use a flat file or bench grinder to smooth down the rivet until it's flush with the upper (convex) side of the spoon. Finish smoothing with fine sandpaper or buffing wheel.

Now, fine-tune the bend in the weed guard so that each of its legs is positioned just forward of the point of the hook and about half an inch on either side of it. Using sharp-nose pliers, bend the weed-guard legs again where they intersect with the hook point. The lower legs of the weed guard should be more or less parallel to the lower bend of the hook and extend just past the barb. (If you're using 2/0 Mustad salmon hooks, the lower legs of the weed guard will be about half an inch long.)

Final spoon, with weed guard to protect hook point.

I've attempted soldering hook and weed guard in place with various types of solder (including silver solder), but have never obtained the strength I wanted without discoloring the spoon with excessive heat. With riveted construction, there's no need to worry about the spoon and its hook parting company while a lunker's on the line.

Getting a Dark Color

Several bass fishermen of my acquaintance like to use a dark-colored spoon in combination with their pork-rind strips, rather than polished or painted brass. The idea, of course, is to attract the fish to the pork-rind trailer rather than the bright spoon itself.

Putting a dark finish on polished brass is easily accomplished by treating your spoon with Birchwood Casey aluminum black, a product intended for touching up shooting irons with aluminum frames. The product works as well on brass as on aluminum, giving a low-luster black finish with virtually no reflective quality. Birchwood Casey products are available at most gun shops and sporting-goods stores that cater to the shooting fraternity.

11. Rod, Reel, and Tackle Repair

Fellows I know who'd no more put their shotguns away without a thorough cleaning than they'd bed down their bird dogs without feeding them think nothing of stacking rods, reels, and tackle in the corner without a second glance. Such practice speaks well of the ruggedness of today's fishing equipment, but it's a poor way to treat articles we expect to perform flawlessly on lake or stream. A pinch of prevention, as they say, is worth a passel of cure.

There's no such thing as tackle that isn't prone to wear, abrasion, and eventual failure. Rods, reels, and other tackle are obviously used in marine environments, and water and sunlight are the natural enemies of metal and fiber. A good rod or reel can cost as much today as did a quality shotgun twenty-five years ago, and who knows where prices will go in the future. Preventive maintenance and speedy repair will keep fishing tackle working years longer.

Many simple repairs of a more or less temporary nature can be made out on the lake as need arises. Other, more difficult or permanent repairs are better made at the workbench after the fish are in the icebox or freezer. In this chapter, I want to discuss both approaches—the temporary expedient as well as the permanent fix. Either way, you'll be money—and pleasurable fishing—ahead.

Repairing Rods

Many a still-useful rod has been relegated to the trash heap because of a splintered shaft, broken handle, or worn guides. Only in a relatively few instances, however, are these maladies incurable, and even when they are it's often possible to use the unbroken parts for other purposes. A rod with a broken butt section, for example, can usually be returned to service after a ferrule is added at the break. Alternatively, the tip section can be converted to ice-fishing duty.

Ferrules, as discussed in Chapter 5, were once made of metal and unduly dampened rod action. Today, glass-to-glass and graphite-to-graphite ferrules are the rule. These not only give better performance than the old metal units, they also simplify installation. Several catalog houses and some local tackle shops sell short lengths of tapered graphite and fiberglass stock used to make up ferrules. This repair stock comes in different tapers, so all you need do is find the one that matches your broken rod section, cut it to length, and epoxy it in place.

Making an attractive job of installing a ferrule requires a perfectly square and clean cut of the rod shaft on either side of the break. It's possible to do the job with a hacksaw and judicious sanding, but the easiest way I've found is to use a tubing cutter. To avoid scarring the blank, place a wrap or two of masking tape on either side of the cutting line. A few turns of the tubing cutter, and the job is done.

Repair ferrules, unlike takedown ferrules, don't require separation, so both rod sections are cemented in place. For added strength as well as appearance, I wrap the entire break area with winding thread after fitting and cementing are done.

Rod tips also get broken, often, it seems, while docking a boat with rods carelessly stowed. Here the cure is to purchase a replacement tip section that matches, as closely as possible, the original rod shaft. If the broken tip belongs to a two-piece rod, replacement usually consists of nothing more than removing guides and tiptop from the old rod section and putting them on the new one.

If the broken tip section belongs to a one-piece rod, the best approach is to cut the rod (with a tubing cutter) about midsection, and make the ferrule installation just described. Alternatively, if you want to convert your rod to a two-piece unit, make your cut at a point on the butt section where the inside diameter equals the outside diameter of the replacement tip. This takes a bit of doing, and it's best to make your initial cut at a slightly smaller (closer to the tip) section than you think may be called for. Successive cuts are made farther down the shaft until just the right diameter is found. Be sure to wrap the butt section with winding thread, for added strength, for an inch or so behind the cut. Also, it's a good idea to plug the hollow end of the tip section with a small piece of rubber or other material to repel water and dirt.

HANDLE REPAIR   One of the attractions of cork handles is the relative ease with which they can be repaired. Most cork rings are supplied in widths of one-half inch, so this becomes your basic unit of repair. If the damaged section is half an inch or less, wrap masking tape on either side of the repair area, half an inch apart. If the repair area is larger than half an inch, space your tape at appropriate locations, but in increments of half-inches.

Now, carefully use an X-acto knife to cut precisely parallel lines along the inside edge of each tape wrap. Cut through the cork handle all the way to the underlying rod blank, then use a small chisel or sharpened screwdriver to remove the damaged section.

Select a cork ring (or rings, as the case may be) that is slightly larger in outside diameter than the handle section you are replacing. With a caliper, measure the diameter of the rod blank where the repair is being made and, if necessary, enlarge (with a rat-tail rasp or file) the holes in the cork ring to this size. Do your rasping over a clean sheet of paper and save the dust. (I'll tell you why in a moment.)

Pick up your X-acto knife again and cut the replacement ring exactly in half. Fit it around the rod blank and glue in place with flexible epoxy or rubber-base contact cement. Now use a rasp and increasingly finer grades of sandpaper to bring the repaired section into conformity with the rest of the handle. If you've made a slight miscalculation and have unsightly seams where the repair was made, mix the cork dust you saved with Duco cement and fill them in. Complete your sanding and the job is done.

Anyone who has fished for very many years has had a guide or tiptop come loose in the middle of a cast or has somehow broken his rod tip just below the tiptop. Every fisherman worth his salt carries tape and a hot-melt glue stick in his tackle box for just such emergencies.

Electrician's tape works for emergency guide repair, but it has the unfortunate affinity for leaving a gummy residue that must be removed before permanent rewrapping can be done. A much better product, made just for the purpose, is a mylar-based tape made by Weber Tackle. It comes in a convenient quarter-inch width, has just the right amount of flex, and is tough as a boot. If you don't object to the appearance, it can be fished for several seasons without coming loose. The better approach, of course, is to rewrap the guide with winding thread at your first opportunity.

Several excellent tiptop replacements are available for those unfortunate but all-too-frequent occasions when we break our rod tips. I once carried several sizes of tiptops in my field repair kit, but still never seemed to have one that was just right for the job at hand. Of late, I've taken to carrying an emergency rod top repair kit made by the Johnny Walker Company over in Detroit. This handy little kit, about the size of a penny matchbox, consists of an outsize tiptop, a spring clip that adjusts its diameter to that of the rod tip, and three shrink tubes that hold everything in place. All you do is trim the broken rod tip, slide one of the shrink tubes over the rod shaft, put the tiptop in place with the spring clip, and heat the shrink tube with your Zippo. In about two minutes you're ready to saddle up and start fishing again.

Repairing Reels

I once considered myself reasonably erudite when it came to reel repair and even picked up a few bucks from time to time puttin' the little darlings back in working order. Right up front, though, I'd best confess I'm no more knowledgeable about the innards of these new computerized models than I am about the workings of an electronic ignition system.

With the probable exception of reels whose functional capabilities apparently rest in the tender hands of LCD readouts and such, it's been my experience that about 90 percent of all reel failures result from improper maintenance and easily remedied malfunctions. Nearly all are well within the abilities of ordinary mortals—if home craftsmen should be so considered—to repair.

For a number of years, I've taught fishing lessons to youngsters down at our local Izaak Walton League chapter. A major attraction of the lessons is that better than half our time is devoted to fishing our amply stocked lakes. Sad to relate, about half the kids show up with reels that I must repair before getting down to the fun of fishing. Very infrequently do I encounter a problem that justifies a trip to a factory-authorized service center.

Relatively few new car buyers sally forth upon the highways without reading the operator's manual that comes with the car. Yet I would

127

venture that less than half the purchasers of new reels look at their instruction manuals until something goes wrong. I'm often reminded of the words of a wise old guide I once fished with down on Toledo Bend. As nearly as I can remember, they went something like this: "There's a helluva difference betwixt education and experience. The first is what you git when you read the instructions that come with your tackle. The second is what you git when you don't."

Reasonable care, frequent lubrication, appropriately sized tools, a clear working area, and thorough reading of the instruction book will enable any moderately dexterous person to keep any of today's better reels in good working order for many years.

Careful and thorough reading of owner's manuals that come with all good reels is one of the keys to keeping them operational.

REEL-REPAIR TOOLS

Some, in fact most, of the parts you'll be working with in cleaning and repairing your reels are quite small, and you should have tools that are appropriately sized for the task at hand. Several reel manufacturers provide small combination screwdriver-wrenches with their products. These are useful for minor repairs, but won't suffice for complete takedowns. Small, hollow-ground screwdrivers such as are used by gunsmiths are well suited for reel repair, and a set of precision (jeweler's) screwdrivers in both blade and Phillips-head configuration are virtually essential. A set of miniature precision nut drivers in various sizes is also well worth the modest price. Increasingly, nut heads are sized in both metric and English units, and the serious reel repairman must be prepared to purchase nut drivers or socket wrenches in both configurations.

REEL CONSTRUCTION

Modern reels are miracles of construction and employ just about every space-age material known to man. Today's reels are lighter, more rugged, and more trouble-free than anything we've known in the past. Moreover, they're downright "user-friendly." By this I mean you no longer need three hands and twelve fingers to fish with them. Graphite is the construction material of choice for many of the new reels, and the metals that are being used, such as titanium, are also lightweight, noncorrosive, and highly durable. In some reels, high-strength plastics such as Lexan and Teflon have replaced metal for certain internal gears.

Improvements in both the composition and construction of line rollers on spinning reels have all but eliminated the line-abrasion problems that once plagued this type of reel, and line pick-up pins have replaced serrated spools on all the better spin-casting models. Five-to-one retrieve ratios, once the exception, have now become the rule, and new helical-cut gears are overcoming the reduced power that once characterized high-speed reels.

For years I've been telling my wife I'd teach her how to use a bait-casting reel once she had mastered her spinning reels. But technology has passed me up, and today's bait casters are so refined that anyone can learn to use them with relative ease. The big thing has been the addition of magnetic braking controls that dampen the spool at the end of the cast and greatly reduce backlash, that old bugbear of us bait-casting enthusiasts.

Of course, the more you dampen your spool, the shorter your cast will be, but once the basics are learned, the sugarfoot can begin to back off on the magnetic control and develop an "educated" thumb like us old-timers learned to do before even mechanical and centrifugal brakes were invented.

With the possible exception of the new computerized reels I mentioned earlier, improvements in reel construction and design haven't complicated them. In fact, just the reverse is true. Not only do modern reels require less frequent repair than did their predecessors, I believe they may be a tad easier to work on.

Frequent lubrication—but *not* excessive lubrication—is the best friend your reel has. A few drops of reel oil during a day's fishing will do wonders, and occasional greasing will keep it hummin' for years. The best of the reel lubes are silicone based, and that's the only kind you should use, either for periodic lubrication or as a replacement grease. Silicone not only possesses greater lubricity than nearly any other material known, it also forms a monomolecular film that repels moisture.

FREQUENT LUBRICATION

Daiwa's pump-type reel greaser greatly simplifies getting into small places.

I've used Garcia's Silicote reel lube for several years and wouldn't leave home without a tube of it stowed in my tackle box. More recently, Daiwa has come out with a pump-type reel greaser that looks like a winner. One of the more helpful aspects of the Daiwa unit is a set of diagrams on the back of its packing card that shows the important lubrication points for bait-casting, spinning, and spin-casting reels. It's worth your while to buy one of the pump greasers just to retain the card for frequent reference.

PERIODIC TAKEDOWN
AND CLEANING

It's not use, but dirt, that causes most reels to fail. Taking a reel apart, cleaning it, replacing the lubricant, and putting it back together again is no more complicated than fixing Mama's toaster. Besides, it will familiarize you with your reel's inner workings and enable you to identify and repair problems if and when they occur.

Depending on frequency and conditions of use, it's a good idea to break down your reel and clean it every couple of years. If you dunk it in the lake a time or two during the fishing season, it's best that you strip and clean it before stowing it away for the winter. (Unless, of course, you're one of those fortunate types who take off for Florida when the first snowflake falls.)

The primary requisite for reel disassembly is a clear working area and an organizational system that assures all parts being replaced in the order they are removed. I've never found anything better for small-parts organization than a couple of Styrofoam egg cartons with the individual cavities numbered sequentially. So armed, and with a schematic diagram that comes packed with all quality reels, you've almost got to work at it to screw up.

A clear working area and a system that assures all parts will be replaced in proper order make it possible for any home craftsman to make many reel repairs without difficulty.

Begin by stripping (and usually junking) all the line of the spool if you haven't recently done so. Then remove the screws or bolts that hold the plates or covers in place. Close at hand you should have a small container (a teacup works fine) half-filled with carbo-chlor (trichloro-ethane). Holding each part with tweezers or small pliers, swish it around in the cleaner until all dirt and lubricant is removed. As each part is cleaned, inspect it for nicks and abrasions that may interfere with its proper function. Minor nicks can be removed with a needle file and emery cloth. Corroded parts (a less frequent occurrence with the materials being used in today's reels) should be cleaned with a mildly abrasive cream such as Wright's silver polish. Gears with broken teeth, screws with stripped threads, and other damaged parts should be replaced, for which you should look to your nearest service center.

Pack each gear, ratchet, spring, bearing, and contact point with a small amount of reel lube (don't overdo it) and reassemble the reel. I guarantee it'll work better and last longer given this kind of care and attention.

Many aspiring fishermen have begun their fishing careers with closed-face or spin-casting reels. While these reels are marvelous little gadgets and extremely easy to master, they are perhaps more prone to minor malfunction than any other type sold. One problem is that, unlike spinning and bait-casting reels, the line is out of sight and consequently out of mind. Wind knots, debris, and dirt picked up by the line are carried into the reel where they immediately begin to cause problems. Many times, failure to cast, or short casts, are nothing more troublesome than the line becoming wrapped around the gears. (This was once a problem with spinning reels as well, but modern skirted spools have just about eliminated it.)

Once line has become enmeshed in reel gears, there's no cure except stripping off the line and replacing it. Because most spin-casting rigs are used by kids whose casts seldom exceed ten or fifteen yards, there's no need to remove all the line. Simply join new line to old with a blood knot and use the old line for backing. I make it a practice to replace the first fifty yards or so of line on all my reels at the beginning of every fishing season. This practice, all by itself, will eliminate a lot of the problems often attributed to reel performance.

CORRECTING LINE PROBLEMS

One of the more common failures associated with open-face (spinning) reels is a malfunctioning bail. Bail problems often result from (1) a bent bail, (2) lost or loose screws holding the bail in place, or (3) a broken or weakened spring that prevents the bail from opening and closing as it should. Before consigning your reel to the service center or stripping it down, check these items and correct them by (1) straightening or replacing the bail; (2) removing the bail screws and retightening them after cleaning and adding a drop of Lock-Tite or Super Glue to their threads; and (3) replacing the bail spring. Only the last requires a minor takedown operation.

PROBLEMS WITH BAILS

The level-wind mechanism seems to be the item that fouls up most often on bait-casting reels. This, I'm sure, is because it is exposed on the front of the reel, and line retrieve can carry debris that lodges in the grooves of the worm shaft. This, of course, prevents the line carriage from trav-

PROBLEMS WITH LEVEL WINDS

131

eling back and forth as it should. A couple of blasts from a spray can of WD-40, followed by a few drops of reel lube, frequently solves the problem in short order. If this doesn't work, use a toothpick to clean the grooves in the worm shaft, an operation that sometimes requires minor disassembly.

If disassembly is required, check also the line carriage pawl and nut. If dirt has been present on the worm shaft for some time, the pawl can become worn from abrasion, and the threads on the nut holding it and the carriage in place can become stripped. If polishing the pawl and/or reseating the nut with Lock-Tite doesn't solve the problem, replacement of the carriage assembly may be necessary.

PROBLEMS WITH DRAGS

Strange to say, I've never had many problems with drags on my reels, possibly because I fish level-wind reels almost exclusively and rely on my thumb more than my drag. Nonetheless, poor drag action is one of the more common problems associated with reels, and, after rotten line, likely the leading cause of lost fish.

Drags, of course, are the mechanisms that determine the amount of pressure necessary to peel line off your reel. As far as I know, all drag systems depend on the friction created by hard (usually soft-metal) washers bearing on ones made of softer material. Felt and leather were once the materials of choice for soft washers, and asbestos and compressed cork have also been used. Many of the newer reels are equipped with Teflon or fiber washers, and each of these materials seems to require different lubrication and maintenance techniques. In the instruction book accompanying your reel, note whether its drag requires lubrication and the recommended frequency of application. Teflon, for example, should be greased only with an antiseize compound, while felt requires frequent oiling to work well.

A fair number of experts claim that oiled leather remains the best material for soft washers, and I suspect they're right. If you want to make leather replacement washers for your reel, the procedure is fairly simple. Visit your local leather shop and select a piece of thin shoe leather that is oil-tanned. Punch holes in it and then use the old washers to trace circles around the holes. Use scissors (curved fingernail scissors work great) to cut out the traced discs.

I've always used light machine (reel) oil to lubricate drag washers, but some guys swear that STP engine additive is better than anything else. Be sure to note the order in which you remove the washers and replace them in the same manner. The usual order is for the hard (metal) and soft washers to be interspersed with one another, but numbers and arrangements can vary.

Another thing I might mention is to back off on your drag setting whenever your reel is stored for any length of time. Constant compression from a hard-set drag can cause soft washers to take on a "set" that results in a jerky drag. Also, be sure to put a drop or two of oil on the drag (assuming your instruction book calls for it) before storing. If you want to be real precise about setting your drag, tie a spring-loaded fish scale to your line and ask a buddy to read it as you put tension on the line and set the drag. Drags should be set at about half the test of the line you've loaded on your reel.

Much of what I've written in previous chapters about making your own lures pertains equally well to their repair. Among the more common lure repairs are repainting, tuning to improve retrieve characteristics, replacing hooks and screw eyes, and tying on new hair, feathers, or other dressings that have been chewed up and become worn through use. I seldom do it myself, but worms and other plastic-bodied lures can be saved, melted down, and remolded.

Nothing's more discouraging than losing a good fish because a screw eye pulls loose or a rusted hook breaks right at the moment of truth. Screw eyes seldom rust or pull out if they are initially set with Duco cement and the lure body properly sealed with a liquid-plastic epoxy to exclude water. Still, occasional inspection and replacement is a worthwhile investment of your time. Wood-bodied plugs will become waterlogged if chipped paint is ignored for long, and this in turn is the most frequent cause of lost and broken screw eyes.

Once a screw eye has been lost or becomes rusted, the best repair calls for plugging the original hole with epoxy or a good cement, painting over the hole, and inserting a replacement screw eye a fraction of an inch fore or aft of the original. Be *sure* that the wood body of the lure is thoroughly dried before repair is undertaken.

Hook replacement is a normal part of fishing, but one that is often overlooked by even the best anglers. Every tackle box should boast a hook-sharpening file or Carborundum stone, but a rusted or badly bent hook should be replaced, not sharpened. The most common cause of rusted hooks is failure to keep your tackle box dry.

Complete reconditioning of a wooden plug begins with removing all hardware, then stripping the paint by brushing on Strypeeze or another good paint remover. These agents can have a devastating effect on Plexiglas diving lips and discolor those made of metal, so be sure to blank off the lips with masking tape before applying paint remover. With paint removed, fill any deep gouges with Plastic Wood or a similar cellulose-fiber filler and sand the body lightly. Give the lure a good coat of epoxy-type liquid plastic or several coats of wood sealer. Then proceed with painting, following the procedures described in Chapter 9.

Spinnerbaits and buzzbaits can usually be reconditioned by straightening their wire parts and replacing hooks, swivels, clevises, and blades. It's possible to recondition blades by painting them, but if you do so, I advise stripping off all existing paint, sanding to obtain tooth, priming, and spraying with auto-body paint. Brush painting spinner blades, in my experience, can inhibit their action.

Who among us has not been out on the lake when the fish are hitting only yellow (or orange or black) lures and the last one we have in that particular color or pattern has just broken off? The obvious solution is to arm ourselves with redundant colors in every lure pattern. But while redundant systems are a necessity for space flight, they can fill a tackle box to overflowing in short order.

A better approach, if one doesn't overdo it, is to go afield with a small kit whose contents enable us to modify the colors, patterns, appearance, and sometimes the action of the lures we normally carry. The selection need not be massive and, indeed, defeats its purpose if it is.

MODIFYING LURES AFIELD

A variety of permanent felt-tip marking pens, plastic tape, lure decorators, and spare spinner blades are basic to a lure-modification kit.

If not included in your regular tackle box, add a sharp knife or razor blade, matches or Zippo lighter, rubber skirts in several colors, and a variety of snaps, swivels, and split rings. No fisherman would take to lake or stream without spare hooks in several sizes and configurations in his tackle box, so we need not include these in our kit.

Among the more useful tapes available to fisherfolk are the diffractive-prism tapes made by Luhr Jensen and others. A small package of this tape, which usually comes in 3-by-3-inch format, contains a variety of colors in designs that refract light. With prism tape, you can modify the colors of spoons, spinner blades, and small plugs. Merely strip off the backing, apply the tape to a *dry* lure, and trim off the excess with a sharp knife or razor blade.

Prismatic tapes and lure decorations are helpful for dressing up plugs and spoons while on the lake or stream.

Lure decorators made by Witchcraft Tackle Company (Box 183, Addison, Illinois, 60101) perform essentially the same function, but are precut in a variety of patterns from ladderbacks to diamonds to lightning designs. Stick-on eyes are available from the same company, and though this may seem a minor addition, they can sometimes make a difference with deep-schooled fish.

Permanent marking pens, available in a variety of colors from art-supply stores, are amazingly waterproof and long-lasting. As noted in an earlier chapter, they can be removed with alcohol. Most waterproof colors are translucent, which means they work best on lighter lures without intricate design patterns. The pens work best on painted lures, but can also be used on spoons by first applying masking tape. The darker shades can also be used to color plastic worms.

Some very basic changes in the colors and configurations of plastic worms can also be made by cutting two worms on a bias, heating the cut ends, and pressing them together until the plastic hardens. An endless variety of patterns, from fire tails to split tails, are possible. Fish them Texas-rigged or as trailers on spinnerbaits or spoons—whatever the fish are hitting.

About the only requisites for on-the-water lure modifications other than a few basic supplies are a fertile imagination and the willingness to experiment. Being the finicky creatures that they are, it's sometimes amazing how fish will strike lures that have been altered only slightly. Try it sometime when the fishing is slow.

It's obvious that major chores such as stripping down reels, repainting lures, and rewrapping guides are best done at the workbench, but there are numerous repairs that can be made afield. The only requirement is that you carry a modest number of suitable tools and a small collection of spare parts. I recommend that these be toted in a small plastic box reserved exclusively for the purpose. Having one on hand can sometimes make the difference between a minor misfortune and a spoiled fishing trip.

An Emergency Repair Kit

A selection of small tools and spare parts is all that is required for an emergency field repair kit that can keep a fishing trip from turning into a disaster.

I've already mentioned the emergency rod tip made by Johnny Walker Company and the mylar guide-wrapping tape sold by Weber Tackle. Both should be included in every emergency repair kit, along with a hot-melt glue stick and tubes of quick-set epoxy cement.

Over the years I've amassed a substantial number of small screws, springs, washers, and similar reel-repair parts that I house in a couple of photographic film canisters and carry in my repair kit. Garcia and other quality reel makers sell a variety of spare parts for the reels they make, and a few of the more frequently needed items should be included in your kit. Particularly useful, in my experience, are such items as bail springs and screws (for spinning reels), drag washers, handle nuts, drive shaft shims, and line-carriage pawls (for bait-casting reels). These and other reel parts come packed in small plastic envelopes, from which they need not be removed until needed.

135

No emergency repair kit can be complete without a can of WD-40, a tube of silicone-based reel lube, and a plastic container of reel oil. Applied frequently but judiciously, lubricants will prevent many problems before they occur.

If you fish with two-piece rods, it's worth your while to carry a small piece of beeswax and a segment of a candle in your emergency repair kit. The beeswax will tighten a loose ferrule and the paraffin will loosen one that's too tight. Kits can get hot and melt these items, so it's good to wrap them individually in small plastic (sandwich) bags or something of the sort.

I can't imagine a tackle box without a pair of sharp-nose pliers. But let me suggest that you go one step further and include a second pair in your repair kit. One of the pliers can be a pair of those nifty combination fisherman's tools that do everything except cook your coffee. A second pair of pliers will prove most welcome when you start tuning a diving lip, straightening a spinnerbait shaft, or repairing a bent bail.

Most good reels come with a combination screwdriver-wrench, and one of these for each reel you plan to fish with are good additions to your emergency repair kit. Unfortunately, many reels also contain a number of small screws that these combination tools won't fit, so a small set of precision screwdrivers should also be carried afield. I definitely do *not* recommend attempting to tear down a reel completely in the field, but occasional tightening of all exposed screws can prevent their loss.

A couple of small needle files are often helpful while afield. In my emergency kit are a flat file, a hook-sharpening file, and a rat-tail file. A small square of sandpaper or emery cloth can be indispensable for any number of purposes, and a square of crocus cloth will remove burrs and grooves from rod guides.

The contents of your emergency repair kit will depend, of course, on the kind of fishing you do. Fly fishermen, for example, will likely want to include a few packets of fly-line cleaner, a splicing needle, and perhaps a tube for tying nail knots. Items will suggest themselves as you go along, and you may find that other items included initially merely take up space. The important thing, as every Boy Scout knows, is "be prepared."

My final suggestion, though it really doesn't figure as part of an emergency repair kit, is that you acquire the habit of carrying spare spools of good-quality monofilament line in several sizes. I don't know why it is, but it seems that half the marinas in the country stock only off-brand line and then charge three prices for it. Buying several spools of quality line, such as Trilene or Sigma, before you take off on your fishing trip is good economy.

For putting new line on your reel while in fishing camp, I highly recommend the Reelminder kit made by Red Eye Tackle Company and available through a number of catalog houses and tackle shops. These little items are helpful for cranking on fresh line in the workshop, and for putting it on while afield they're darn near indispensable.

Line often becomes twisted during a day's fishing, especially if trolling is included in your agenda. To overcome this sometimes frustrating problem, remove all terminal gear from your line and let it (the line, that is) trail out behind your boat on the way back to dock. This will take every twist out of the line and leave it in good shape for the next day's fishing.

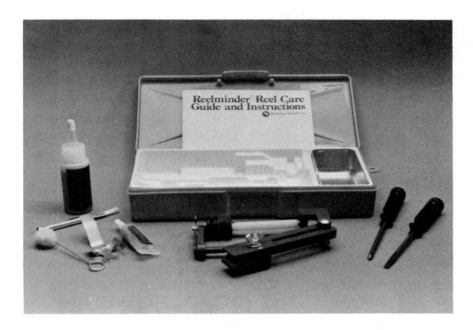

Red Eye Tackle Company's Reelminder kit is helpful for reel maintenance and, according to the author, indispensable for putting line on reels while in fishing camp.

12. Accessories You Can Make

Back in what some folks like to think of as the "good ol' days," before Teflon and polypropylene and all the other tough-as-nails plastics were invented, lots of us made all sorts of fishing gear out of wood and whatever other materials we could scrounge.

Wood, to my thinking, is still a lot better-looking than molded plastic, but I think even the most conservative among us must admit it's usually not as functional for fishing tackle. A custom-crafted wooden tackle box, for example, is a darn sight prettier than one of modern plastic, yet weighs more and won't take one-tenth the abuse before falling to pieces.

Had I written this book a couple of decades ago, I'd likely have included plans for building a tackle box of wood, weaving a landing net of cotton or nylon cord, and perhaps crafting a minnow trap of wood and wire. Today, however, given the low-cost availability of better products than we can make, few such endeavors are worthwhile. This is, after all, a how-to-do-it book for practical fishermen, and practicality demands that anything we make be either better or cheaper (and hopefully both) than what we can buy off the shelf.

With these few caveats out of the way, let's move along to a few selected accessory items that can be undertaken cheaply or work better than manufactured goods.

An Economical Rod Rack

Literally scores of rod racks molded of hard rubber and plastic are on the market today. One such rack suspends six rods from the roof of my pickup cap. Few commercial racks, however, have the eye appeal of a wall-mounted wooden rack that holds your rods upright, the preferred position for long-term storage. A wooden rack is especially appealing for the den or summer cottage, where rods are often racked next to the door for immediate use.

You can build the rack described here in an afternoon, using basic hand tools. Power tools will obviously speed up the job somewhat, but they're not essential. To build a rack that will hold five casting rods with reels attached, begin with two pieces of 1-by-4-inch white pine sawed to 34-inch lengths. You'll also need two ¾-inch dowels in conventional 36-inch lengths. When you buy your dowels, try to find ones without doglegs in them—not as simple a task as one might think.

On both boards, mark and drill ¾-inch holes for the dowels that are centered as to width (i.e., 2 inches from each edge of your one-by-fours) and 1½ inches from the ends of each board. Each of these four holes will be drilled halfway through the thicknesses of the boards, or about ⅜ inch deep. (More about drilling blind holes in a moment.)

Also on both boards, come in five inches from each end and mark perpendicular lines on their faces. Now mark three more perpendicular lines, spaced six inches apart, for a total of five lines along the face of both boards.

On the board that will form the lower shelf of your rod rack, mark points 1½ inches from the front edge of the board on each perpendicular line. These points will be the centers for 1½- or 2-inch blind holes you will now drill halfway through the upper face of the lower shelf. These holes, which will be lined with felt or sheet cork, will provide support for the rod handles and prevent their slipping out of the rack.

Upright Wall-Mounted Rod Back

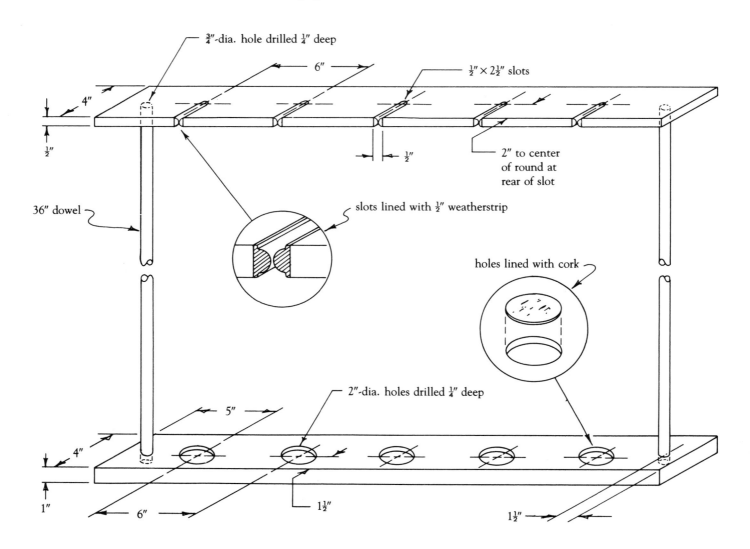

Now, about those blind holes you must drill. This is the hardest part of building the rack unless you have Forstner bits designed for the purpose. These are usually special-order tools and cost $15 to $30 apiece. This is a pretty steep price unless you're in the blind-hole business, so I alter spade bits to do the job by grinding down their points until only stubs remain. Spade bits, especially in the larger diameters, are notorious for chewing up wood where you don't want it chewed, and some judicious sanding around the circumferences of your blind holes will likely be required.

To obtain a 2-inch diameter hole that's free of blemished wood around its edges, I drill a 1½-inch hole, then finish it to a 2-inch diameter using a sanding drum mounted on a Dremel Moto-Tool. A sanding disc mounted on a Dremel tool works equally well for smoothing out the bottoms of the blind holes. This part of the job takes longer than everything else combined, but for me it's preferable to spending big bucks for a flat-bottom drill bit I seldom use.

Drilling blind holes for rod rack.

After completing the blind holes in your lower shelf, turn to the board that will form your upper shelf. Measure in 2½ inches from the front edge, along the perpendicular lines you drew earlier, and drill ½-inch holes all the way through the board at these points. These will form the back walls of the slots you will cut (using a saber or coping saw) to house the shafts of your rods.

Before assembling, sand the boards and dowels with increasingly finer grades of sandpaper until a smooth finish is obtained. Glue the dowels in place in the ¾-inch blind holes you've drilled for them, clamping both upper and lower shelves with pipe clamps until the glue has set. If

141

you use a good quality carpenter's glue such as Elmer's Professional, no screws or nails will be required. With your clamps secured, check everything with a carpenter's square to be sure you've achieved perpendicular alignment.

After allowing the glue to set overnight, give the assemblage a final sanding and stain with a color of your choice. Follow the staining directions on the can, then complete the finish with a couple of coats of good varnish. As your final step, use rubber-base contact cement to glue foam-rubber weather stripping in the upper-shelf slots (to retain and protect your rods) and sheet cork in the lower holes that hold the rod handles. Affix hangers on the back edge of the top shelf, mount your rack on the wall, and display your rods attractively.

This simple-to-make rod rack is more attractive than most commercial models made from plastic and can accommodate up to five casting or spinning rods in an upright position.

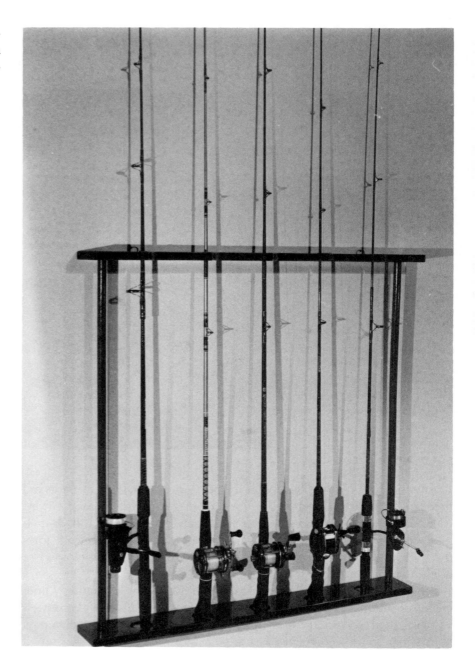

This basic design can be modified to hold more or fewer rods. Also, if you plan to rack spinning or fly rods, rather than casting rods with their larger reels, you can space the rods a little closer together. Altogether, it's an afternoon's work of which you'll be proud.

An Indestructible Rod Case

Now that we've made somethin' purty, we're gonna make something that's ugly as sin but practical as pockets on a fishing vest. Living as I do in Illinois but being addicted to southern bass fishing, many of my fishing trips begin with a plane ride. You've heard the horror stories about how airline luggage handlers vie to see who can inflict the most damage on sporting equipment. So I'll spare you the gory details. Suffice it to say I'll gladly match you tale for tale.

I own several commercial rod cases, but nothing I've found equals the indestructibility of PVC (polyvinylchloride) sewer pipe. Cases made from this stuff will frustrate the attentions of any gorilla the airlines ever hired. Granted, a rod case made from it ain't the classiest-looking thing that ever came down a runway, but maybe that's part of its charm.

Three-inch pipe seems to be the size best suited to the pistol-grip casting rods I usually carry, but a smaller diameter will likely suffice if your usual traveling rods are used for spinning or fly-fishing. PVC pipe, which comes in ten-foot lengths, can be bought at most building-supply outlets. Besides a length of pipe, you'll need a can of special PVC cement and two each of the following: connector sleeves, threaded (female) adapters, and threaded (male) plugs. The tab for the whole works will run about twenty bucks, so we're not talking economy here, just protection.

Begin your construction by hacksawing the pipe to whatever length necessary to encase the longest rod shaft you plan to carry by plane. After sawing, smooth down the rough edges with a file. The sleeves are used to connect the female adapters to the pipe, so smear a healthy dose of PVC cement over all surfaces to be joined. The male plugs then screw into the threaded adapters. One of the plugs can be cemented permanently in place after lining it with sponge rubber to protect your rods. For added protection, I suggest that you ask the wife to stitch up some individual rod bags out of cotton flannel.

I haven't deemed it necessary, but you can pretty up your rod case by painting it or wrapping it with Con-Tact brand self-adhesive covering. A wood-grain finish of the latter really looks nice and might even survive two or three plane trips. You can also add nylon webbing for a carrying strap by doubling it over at the ends and affixing it to the case with pop rivets.

A Low-Cost Lure Retriever

Nothing's more frustrating than hanging up a good deep-diving lure on a submerged tree limb or heavy brush, especially if it has been taking fish. There are several good lure retrievers on the market, but you can make your own from stuff you likely have around the house and in your tackle box.

To begin, assemble a large split ring (the kind used for key rings), an old chain dog leash, and a length of strong nylon cord. From your tackle box, take a 2- or 3-oz. bank sinker, a couple of ½-oz. teardrop sinkers and two No. 5 split rings. Dog chains are good because they're

143

relatively heavy and chromed to resist rust. Cut the chain into four 10-inch lengths and slip the end links of two of them onto the split ring. Now put the large sinker on the split ring and add the other two lengths of chain.

Put the small split rings on the other ends of two of the lengths of chain and add the ½-oz. teardrop sinkers to provide a little added weight. Now tie a bowline knot (see Appendix A) in one end of your braided nylon cord (which should be about 25–30 feet long, depending on the water depths you usually fish), and put the resulting loop onto the large split ring along with the chain lengths and bank sinker.

A lure retriever that works as well as most commercial models can be made from a dog chain and items you have in your tackle box.

In use, position your boat over the hang-up and fit the split ring onto your fishing line ahead of your rod tip. Crank your line tight and let the retriever slide down the line as fast as it will go. It will often knock the lure loose when it hits. If not, jiggle the cord until one or more of the retriever chains engages the hooks of your lure, then retrieve with a steady pull. (If your fishing buddy isn't hauling fish out of the same brush pile you're snagged on, he may be willing to crank in your line while you bring your lure aboard.)

I can't honestly say it's a never-fail method, but at least it beats cutting off a good lure without trying. I once brought up two other lures with the same piece of brush mine was snagged on. Turned out to be the best catch of the day.

Styrofoam Marker Buoys

One of the problems inherent in a book like this is that you risk writing too much, telling too little, and boring your readers to death. This next project is sorta borderline, but nobody can say ol' Uncle Jim ain't comprehensive.

Those of us who became early advocates of deep-structure fishing found it necessary to make our own marker buoys from cork or balsa. Nowadays, excellent marker buoys made from polypropylene are available commercially, and Styrofoam is the material of choice for those who still make their own.

By far the quickest and easiest way to cut Styrofoam is with a hot wire. Floral shops and others who use the material frequently work with hot-wire tools that are heated electrically like a soldering iron. It hardly behooves you to buy one of these gadgets, but stainless-steel leader wire stretched across a coping-saw frame and heated with a propane torch works nearly as well. Alternatively, use a sharp filleting knife.

Styrofoam is cut with a sharp knife or hot wire to form body of marker buoy.

From a block of Styrofoam like that packed with many appliances, trim a piece about 6 inches long and 2½ inches square. Cut slots in the center of the block on two sides and round off corners all the way around so the buoy will revolve easily in the water. Now use a rasp or coarse sandpaper to smooth and contour the body until it resembles a squared-off doggy bone.

Styrofoam, of course, is soft and easily indented, so to protect the center section where line will be wound, wrap the foam with a couple of thicknesses of electrician's tape. Alternatively, and to protect the entire buoy from breakage, the whole thing can be coated with Plasti Dip.

Marker buoy is coated with Plasti Dip to make Styrofoam rigid and damage-proof.

145

Instead of dipping the buoy as you do with jigs and smaller objects, apply the Plasti Dip with a soft-bristle brush. Plasti Dip shrinks as it dries, so brush it on in two or three light applications; otherwise, its shrinkage will deform the Styrofoam.

If you use yellow Plasti Dip, no further finish is required. If not, spray paint the buoy with yellow or fluorescent orange paint. Now tie about fifty feet of braided fishing line (thirty-pound test is about right) around the center section of the buoy and fix a lead weight on the other end.

Wrap the line around the waist of the buoy and secure it and the weight with a heavy rubber band until you're ready to mark structure. The weight should be heavy enough to unwind the line when the buoy's thrown overboard and keep it from drifting even in a chop. An old wheel weight works fine.

Finished marker buoy, painted bright yellow and with line and weight attached.

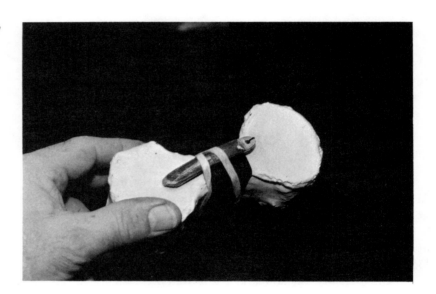

A Simple Live-Bait Box

I seldom use live bait myself (except when the walleyes refuse to hit plastic grubs or in-line spinnerbaits), but several years ago I built a minnow box for a buddy who has a summer cabin up in northern Wisconsin. He says it's been tied to his dock every summer since.

The trouble with a lot of the bait boxes I've seen is that they're elaborate affairs put together with sticks and screen wire all around. They fall to pieces after a few seasons in the water. This one you can make from scrap lumber in less than an hour, and except for minor repairs, it will be around as long as you are.

Start off with a couple of two-by-tens about three feet long and two one-by-fours about 18 inches long (size can vary according to your needs). Mark off 4 inches across the end of each two-by-ten and then cut two corners from each board by measuring a diagonal from a point about 8 inches from the end of the board to your 4-inch mark. This will give you an angled cut of 20 degrees (more or less). Now use galvanized nails to nail the one-by-fours onto the ends of the two-by-tens to form the frame of your bait box.

Scrounge around the workshop or garage until you find a one-by-twelve (or ¾-inch marine plywood) that can be cut into three 18-inch lengths.

Nail two of these boards onto the top edges of the two-by-tens so that they overlap the end pieces (the one-by-fours) by ¼ inch or so. (The important thing is to be sure you leave a ¼-inch gap on either side of the door so you can open it after the wood swells.)

The third 18-inch one-by-twelve becomes a door by hitching one side of it to a nailed-down one-by-twelve with a couple of brass hinges and putting one or two butterfly latches on the other side. Now turn the box over and staple or nail ¼-inch-mesh hardware cloth (down in Texas we call it hail wire) all across the bottom. Use brass staples if you can find them, or galvanized roofing nails if you can't.

Turn the box back over and finish it off by adding a brass or wooden knob to lift the door and a screw eye to tie your bait box to the dock or bank. That's all there is to it.

A Simple Live-Bait Box

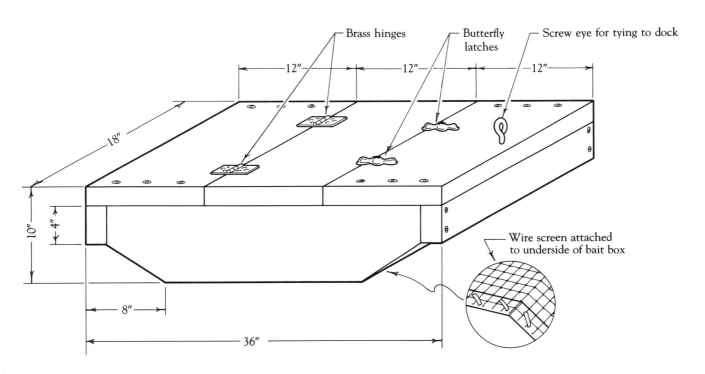

147

13. Handy Tips
to Save You Bucks

This chapter is sort of an afterthought. For the past several years, partially in preparation for writing this book, I've been collecting and jotting down all sorts of ideas for homemade tackle and accessories suggested by friends or dreamed up by yours truly. Some of them I've tried, others I haven't. Some are practical, others less so. Anyhow, I thought I'd use this final chapter to share them with you. Let's jump right in.

This idea came about a few summers back when the wife and I were out bass fishing and not doing much good. But big bluegill were hitting like crazy, so we made a fast trip back to the marina for a carton of red worms. Lo and behold, when we got back to the honey hole, I found my tackle box didn't contain a single bobber, which my wife likes to use for panfishing.

    What I did have on board was a few rolls of 35-millimeter film, packed as usual in ubiquitous little plastic canisters. I removed the film from one canister, held the open end up to my wife's line and popped the top on over the line. It solved the problem beautifully. After doing a little experimenting, I've found that the canisters, partly filled with water, make pretty good casting weights when using light lures in a brisk wind.

    As an additional thought, it occurs to me that a bit of yellow spray paint would make the canisters more visible and thus enhance their utility as bobbers.

I've previously remarked on the use of permanent felt-tip marking pens for touching up lures in the field. Another use to which I've put mine is to mark line length when trolling without benefit of downriggers. All you need do is have a pen with dark-color ink clipped in your fishing vest pocket. When you get a strike, mark the line at the reel. Upon landing your fish, return line to the water until your mark comes up, thereby assuring that your lure will continue running at the same depth you caught your fish.

A few years back, when up in northern Wisconsin on one of my infrequent fly-fishing trips, I noticed one of my buddies spraying something

Film-Canister Bobbers

Marking Trolling Line

Waterproof Flies

on his dry flies. Upon inquiring, I was told that the spray was nothing but Scotchgard, the same stuff used to waterproof fishing jackets and such. He claimed it was the best thing he's found for keeping drys on top of the water. For sure, it's a lot cheaper than specialty products sold for the same purpose. Scotchgard leaves a powdery residue on the flies, but this is easily brushed off after the water repellant dries.

Dowel-Rod Crappie Rig

My mother is an inveterate crappie angler, sitting for hours at night on a lighted fishing dock equipped with multiple-hook crappie rigs. I get bored pretty quickly doing this kind of fishing, so I sometimes wander around the dock observing other fisherfolk.

One idea I liked was a homemade hook harness that used ¼-inch dowels about 5 inches long to spread the hooks. A light teardrop sinker was tied to the end of the harness line, followed by a swivel about 3 inches up the line, followed by the first of two dowels. Another 8 or 10 inches up the line was another swivel followed by another dowel. Each of the dowels had three small (³⁄₃₂-inch) holes drilled in it, one in the center for the main harness line and one in each end for the dropper lines. Up the rig another 4 or 5 inches from the top dowel was a loop (bowline or overhand) knot that was swivel-snapped to the fishing line.

The fisherman had used 8-lb. test monoline for stringing the dowels together and 4-lb. test line for droppers. I think that perhaps the use of single-strand leader wire instead of 8-lb. test mono might make the rig even more effective. As it was, the thing that impressed me about this homemade crappie rig was that it seemed to get tangled (from baitfish swimming around) a lot less frequently than did the commercial crappie rigs the rest of us were using. When I again go night fishing for crappie, I intend to have a couple of these dowel-rod harness rigs in my tackle box.

Reversed Spoons

Last summer when I was up in Wisconsin, most of the northern pike being caught were coming out of heavy beds of cabbage weeds growing along the shore. Red-and-white spoons are acknowledged killers for these toothy critters, but casting a spoon into cabbage weeds is a surefire way to spend a lot of your time hung up. I noticed one fellow in a nearby boat ripping what appeared to be an ordinary spoon through the weeds without any apparent problem. Curious, I pulled alongside and asked him his secret.

He reeled in and swung his lure over to me to look at. What he had done was ingenuity at its simplest: He'd merely reversed the hook and line tie on his spoon, making it ride higher in the water and skim over the weed tops. It didn't take me but a couple of minutes to get out my split-ring pliers and do the same. I spent the next couple of days (all that was left of my vacation) shagging northern out of those weed beds with far fewer hang-ups.

Help From the Ladies

Discounting the obvious camaraderie, there are other advantages to fishing with the ladies. Several times I've made use of items my wife carries in her makeup kit to make emergency tackle repairs. Hard-As-Nails nail polish puts a tough coating on guide windings and jig wrappings, and also can be used to dress up spoons and spinnerbaits. Clear nail enamel can be used to repair dings in wooden plugs that would otherwise admit water.

The stuff they call oily nail-polish remover makes a pretty fair lubricant for frozen screws when it's necessary to field-strip reels, and will also unstick balky metal ferrules. (Don't use it on glass or graphite ferrules.) Those little two-grit emery boards the gals use to shape their nails work pretty good as emergency hook sharpeners and for cleaning up corroded tackle. I've also used them for cleaning plugs on my motor and for corroded battery terminals.

Finally, Vaseline Intensive Care hand lotion is the best stuff I've found for keeping hands from chapping and cracking after several days on the water. It has a permanent place on board our bass boat, thanks to the little woman.

Fine-Tuning Trolled Lures

Plugs that seem to retrieve without problems when casting can prove troublesome at trolling speeds. Sometimes merely bending the line tie can cure the problem.

If your lure wants to run to the right, use a pair of sharp-nosed pliers to bend the line-tie screw eye to the left (as you look at the lure head on). If it runs to the left, bend the line tie to the right.

If your lure wobbles and acts like it wants to turn over, bend the line tie forward and away from the diving lip. For more involved lure tuning, refer to the chapter on plug making.

A Floating Fish Stringer

The boat I have now has live wells fore and aft that keep my catch in good shape until I'm ready to fillet or release them. But for many years I used one of the familiar snap-type chain stringers. Like just about everyone else, I suppose, I've occasionally forgotten to pull the stringer on board when moving down the lake—a memory lapse that has twice resulted in the loss of a stringer full of fish.

If you use a stringer and want to keep this from happening (again?) to you, pick up an ordinary plastic or brass toilet-tank float at the hardware store. Bring the float home and spray-paint it yellow or blaze orange. Next time your stringer comes undone, all you need do is retrace your route until you see that big yellow object bobbing along in the water.

While we're on the subject of stringers, let me urge you to string your fish through both lower and upper lips, not just through the lower lips as is usually done, and never, ever through the gills. You'll find that your fish will live longer.

Slip-Proof Waders

I use chest waders and hip boots more often for duck hunting than for fishing, but I see no reason why this idea shouldn't be equally applicable to fishing situations.

One of the problems with waders and boots is that they tend to slip on your feet, especially when you're going through mucky bottoms. To solve the problem, cut ½- or ¾-inch bands from an old inner tube. Slide the band over your boot at the ankle, stretch it and make a half turn over your instep, then bring the band back down over the toe of your boot. Slide the lower portion of the band back under your arch and march through the muck without a slip.

Rubber-Band Weed Guard

I have an aversion to weed guards, believing that they result in lost strikes. Nevertheless, I have a friend who regularly rigs his single-barb hooks with rubber-band weed guards and somehow manages to catch about as many fish as I do. I'll pass along his method without further comment.

What he does is buy a box of small (one-inch) bands, for which he pays about a buck. He slips a rubber band through the eye of a hook, loops it back through itself, and stretches it down until it engages the barb of his hook. To stay in place, the band obviously has to be stretched fairly tight. My friend claims the rubber bands work better than hooks made weedless by more conventional wire or fiber guards and seldom interfere with setting the hook on a strike.

Velcro Rod Straps

For years I've used pipe cleaners to keep my two-piece rods held together while in transit. They work fine.

Recently, however, I've discovered Velcro, those little toothed strips used for zippers or whatever. My wife found some for me at the local sewing center. Cut into five-inch lengths and wrapped around a rod at both tip and handle, they're a whole lot quicker to secure and remove than pipe cleaners.

The only problem I've had is that a few of them blew off the console of my boat while moving down the lake last fall. This season, I plan to glue a patch of Velcro up under the console where it'll be out of the way. Then I'll simply stick the rod strips to it when they're not holding my rod pieces together.

Straightening Twisted Monoline

Here's one final tip I thought nearly every fisherman was familiar with, but down in southern Illinois last year I fished with a pretty fair angler who greeted it as though he'd just discovered the Holy Grail. Maybe it will be new to you, too.

It's not nearly as bad about it as it once was (thanks to vastly improved line), but monofilament fishing line tends to take on a "set" after it has been spooled for a while. The problem is particularly bothersome early in the season, when line coming off the real wants to coil around itself rather than moving smoothly through the guides.

There's a simple cure, and it's no more complicated than cutting a small (say, two-by-four-inch) patch from a rubber inner tube. If you're fishing from the bank, cast out as far as your kinked line will go, then crank it back in while holding the rubber patch firmly doubled over it just ahead of your reel. With two or three successive casts retrieved through the rubber patch, each of which will be longer as the coils disappear from your line, your line will become straight as an arrow.

The procedure is even easier if you're fishing from a boat. Just let your line flow out behind the boat (without any terminal gear on the line) as you move down the lake. Reel your line back through the rubber patch one time, and the job will be done.

Appendix A. Tackle-Making Terms and Diagrams

Aberdeen—A popular style of hook, widely used in jig making, that is made from relatively soft steel wire that bends instead of breaking.

Acetate floss—A special thread made from an acetate material, used for tying dressing on jigs and other lures. A special solvent, supplied with the thread, is applied after tying is completed and causes the floss to fuse together.

Action—A term used to identify the point at which a rod bends or "unloads" its stored power when casting or fighting a fish. Action is usually described as being "fast," "slow," and so forth.

Aluminum oxide—A hard synthetic material used by several manufacturers as the ring (line-bearing surface) in rod guides.

Attractor tubing—Small-diameter plastic tubing slipped over the shank of the treble hook to attract strikes. The tubing is available in several colors, with red being the most popular.

Ball-bearing swivel—A method of swivel construction in which tiny ball bearings are used as load-bearing surfaces to impart greater strength and torque. More expensive than barrel swivels, they are used for trolling and other situations where line twist is a major problem. *(See Barrel swivel.)*

Bank sinker—A teardrop-shaped sinker with hexagonal sides designed for use in rocky areas, where they resist hanging up somewhat better than other types.

Barrel swivel—The most commonly used type of swivel, in which two looped wires, forming eyes, are joined by a central retainer, the shape of which resembles a barrel.

Basswood—An extremely clear (without grain) and relatively soft hardwood often used in making wooden plugs. Other favorite woods for plug construction are white cedar and white or sugar pine.

Beads—Usually round but sometimes elliptical and/or faceted bits of colored glass, plastic, or metal with holes through their centers used as components in spinnerbait construction. Beads serve both to attract fish and to enhance lure action.

Blank—1) The shaft of a rod before handle assembly, guides, and other components are added; 2) A small piece of metal, usually brass, from which a spoon is forged; 3) A lure before hooks and other hardware are added.

Blank mold—An aluminum mold sold without cavities or sprue holes that enables tackle makers to design their own molded lures.

Bobbin—A small device made of spring steel or heavy wire, used to contain a spool of winding thread and prevent its unwinding while dressing flies, jigs, or other artificial lures. Bobbins can be purchased, or made simply by bending a length of coat-hanger wire to appropriate size.

Body—A center-drilled piece of solid metal (usually brass or steel, but also painted lead) that fits onto the shaft of an in-line spinnerbait to provide form and weight; sometimes refers to the molded-lead portion of jigs and spinnerbaits.

Boron—In fishing-tackle parlance, a man-made fiber used in the manufacture of rod blanks. Boron fiber is produced by reducing a boron-containing gas in contact with a heated filament, usually an alloy of tungsten.

Bucktail—Originally used with specific reference to a jig dressed with hair from the tail of a deer; now more commonly used as a generic description of any lure whose hooks are concealed or disguised with any type of natural or artificial hair. *(See Jigs.)*

Bullet sinker—A type of slip sinker commonly used with plastic worms, the configuration of which is conical or bullet shaped. *(See Slip sinker.)*

Butt cap—A small metal or plastic cap, resembling a chair or crutch tip, that fits over the handle in most types of rod construction (the notable exception being molded-plastic pistol-grip handles used on casting rods).

Butt ferrule—A ferrule applied to the butt end of rod blanks (especially casting rods) that fits into a collet in the rod handle. In recent years, butt ferrules have lost favor among knowledgeable fishermen, who prefer the more sensitive "through-the-handle" type of construction.

Butt grip—In casting and spinning rod construction, that portion of the handle assembly behind the reel seat; the portion of the rod handle by which the rod is gripped.

Butt section—In two-piece rod construction, the larger and heavier portion of the blank. Also, more generally, the lower section of any rod, including the handle assembly.

Butt-wind tape—A flat, narrow tape of woven nylon used in place of winding thread to apply the decorative butt wrap on a rod blank. *(See Winding thread; Butt wrap.)*

Butt wrap—Winding thread or butt-wind tape wound around the butt section of a rod blank just forward of the handle assembly. Butt wrap is purely decorative, and the diamond wrap is the most commonly used pattern. *(See Diamond wrap.)*

Buzzbait—A specialized top-water lure used primarily by southern bass fishermen; characterized by a delta-shaped blade that fits over the upper shaft of the lure.

Carboloy—A trademarked (by General Electric) word used to identify rod-guide rings made of tungsten carbide. *(See Guide ring.)*

Cement—In tackle-making parlance, any of several types of thermal-setting adhesive used to join components used in the construction of rods, lures, and other tackle.

Clevis—A small U-shaped piece of wire or folded metal used to attach spinner blades to the wire shaft of a spinnerbait. In use, the clevis is passed through the hole in the blade and the spinnerbait shaft is passed through holes in each end of the clevis. *(See Stirrup; Folded clevis.)*

Coil-spring fastener—A small loop of concentrically coiled spring wire used to secure the terminal (hook) loop of an in-line spinnerbait.

Collar—In molded jig construction, a cylindrical extension of the jig head or body around which hair or other dressing is tied to conceal or to disguise the hook.

Collet—A device much like the chuck of a drill that is tightened over a male butt ferrule to hold the rod's shaft and handle together. *(See Butt ferrule.)*

Colorado blade—A type of spinner blade, often used for safety-pin spinnerbait construction, that is relatively wide in relation to its length. The configuration of a Colorado blade resembles that of a teardrop.

Color preserver—A clear liquid with a waterlike consistency that is applied to guide wraps to prevent varnish from discoloring the winding thread; sometimes referred to as color preservative.

Core pin—In slip-sinker construction, a small steel rod that is inserted into the mold to form a center hole through which the fishing line is passed. *(See Slip sinker.)*

Cork rings—Round cork washers, usually one-half inch thick, used to make rod handles and sometimes reel-seat bushings. Cork rings are available in several inside and outside diameters, depending upon intended use. *(See Handle; Reel-seat bushing.)*

Crimping pliers—Special-purpose, usually heavy-duty, pliers used to crimp leader sleeves; most crimping pliers also have wire-cutting surfaces.

Cross-line swivel—A swivel with three wire loops, used for hanging drop-line sinkers in trolling and other special-purpose applications.

Diamond wrap—A commonly used decorative butt-wrap pattern consisting of thread wound so as to form interlocking diamond designs. *(See Butt wrap.)*

Dressing—Material tied over the hook of a jig or other lure to conceal and disguise the hook. Commonly used dressing materials include real and artificial hair, tinsel, feathers, and rubber filaments. Jigs that are to be dressed must have collars for the purpose. *(See Collar.)*

Egg sinker—A type of slip sinker used by some worm fishermen, characterized by its egg-shaped configuration. *(See Slip sinker.)*

E-glass—For many years, the fiberglass material of choice for fishing-rod construction; in quality rods, it has been replaced by S-glass in recent years *(See S-glass.)*

Epoxy—A bonding agent composed of polymide or amine resin, to which is added a hardening agent that causes a chemical reaction to occur. Epoxies are the most permanent of the adhesives available to tackle makers.

Ferrule—A two-part (male and female) device used to join the sections of two-piece rods. In modern rod construction, ferrules are composed of the same material (glass or graphite) from which the rod blank is constructed. Most ferrules today are installed by the manufacturer.

Fiberglass—A man-made material that for many years was the best available for rod construction. Fiberglass is made by flowing molten glass through orifices in a melting furnace. *(See E-glass; S-glass.)*

Flash—Excess lead that leaks out of the cavities of two-piece molds. Flashing occurs when the two halves of the mold are not in perfect alignment, or when the halves are not held tightly together when lead is poured into the mold.

Fly-tying scissors—Small, pointed scissors with large finger holes used for clipping hair, thread, and other materials used in tying flies, jigs, and other artificials.

Folded clevis—A type of clevis made from a stamped sheet-metal washer folded in half so that holes are formed at the fold for the insertion of a spinnerbait shaft. *(See Clevis; Stirrup clevis.)*

Foregrip—In casting- and spinning-rod construction (but not fly-rod construction), the portion of the handle assembly forward of the reel seat. *(See Handle.)*

French spinner—A type of spinner blade characterized by a raised center dome on its convex side that causes water to cavitate and create bubbles. *(See Spinner blade.)*

Gimbal—A solid metal butt cap on the handle of heavy offshore rods. The bottom of the gimbal is slotted to receive a bar fitted in the gimbal socket, which is attached to a fighting chair or a belt worn by the fisherman.

Gluing jig—In cork-ring rod-handle construction, a simple, usually handmade clamp used to compress the rings as the cement with which they have been glued together is allowed to cure.

Graphite—A man-made fiber now used extensively in the manufacture of rod blanks. Graphite fiber is produced by passing a polymer filament through a heated vacuum until only carbon atoms remain.

Guide—A device consisting essentially of a hardened ring with metal supporting brackets and a foot, designed to cause the fishing line to flow smoothly and effortlessly along the rod shaft. *(See Guide ring.)*

Guide foot—The portion of a guide that is affixed to the rod blank by windings. Guides usually have two feet, but single-foot guides are increasingly popular for use on ultra-light rods. *(See Windings.)*

Guide ring—The line-bearing surface of a rod guide; modern materials used in guide-ring construction, all of which are extremely hard, include silicon carbide, aluminum oxide, and tungsten carbide. *(See Carboloy.)*

Guide wrapping—The process whereby guides are affixed to the rod blank with winding thread. Wrappings (plural) is a synonomous term for windings.

Handle—A general term usually taken to include the entire handle assembly of a rod, consisting of butt grip and foregrip, reel seat, reel-seat bushing, butt cap, and winding check.

Head cement—A clear, fast-drying cement used over winding thread when tying jigs, flies, and other lures. Cement is never used over guide windings.

Hinged mold—A two-piece mold, usually made of aluminum alloy, held together at one end by hinges and having handles at the other. *(See Pin mold.)*

155

Hook hanger—A small metal device (usually chromed steel) used by some plug manufacturers to affix hooks to the body of a lure. Hook hangers are held on the lure body by tiny, slotted screws. Their use is not as popular as it once was, as they have been replaced by hangers molded into the bodies of plastic lures and by screw eyes and split rings used with wooden plugs.

Hosel—A winding check, usually of somewhat elongated design and larger dimensions, used on heavy rods, or for decorative purposes on smaller rods.

Indiana blade—A type of spinner blade, often used for in-line spinnerbait construction, that is pear shaped in configuration. *(See Spinner blade.)*

Injection mold—In tackle-making parlance, a type of two-piece mold used in making soft-bodied (plastic) lures. A plunger is used to inject hot plastisol forcefully into the mold cavity, after which the mold is unscrewed or unclamped and the lure removed. Simple injection molds have recently become available to home craftsmen, enabling them for the first time to mold round-bodied lures.

In-line spinnerbait—A spinnerbait in which all components—blades, body, attractor beads, and such—are affixed on a single wire shaft that forms the axis of the lure.

Jig—An artificial lure consisting of a lead head or body, into which a specialized (jig) hook is molded. More than thirty different styles of jigs have been developed for a variety of fishing applications, and new variations are being developed every year.

Jig hook—A specialized hook that is molded into the body of a jig. It is characterized by having a sharp (90-degree) bend in its shank just below the eye.

June-bug spinner—A type of spinner blade characterized by a midsection cutout, which forms an arm that fits over the shaft of an in-line spinnerbait in place of a clevis. June-bug spinners are also used as attractors in conjunction with live-bait fishing.

Keeper ring—A small-diameter wire shaped like a winged U that is wrapped onto the rod blank just ahead of the foregrip. It is used to retain the hook or lure while the rod is in transit or otherwise not in use. Also called a "hook keeper."

Lindy sinker—A type of slip sinker popular with walleye fishermen for use with minnows and other live bait; also known as a "walking" sinker. *(See Slip sinker.)*

Line—In modern tackle-making parlance, monofilament nylon or braided Dacron. Lines are available in many tensile strengths, designated as "test," and expressed numerically in pounds. *(See Test.)*

Line tie—The screw eye (in plug construction) or wire loop (in spinnerbait construction) to which the fishing line is attached, either by direct knot or intermediate swivel snap. Sometimes referred to as a "tie loop."

Master wrap—The windings that hold the guides on a rod blank. *(See Butt wrap; Trim wrap; Underwrap.)*

Mold—In tackle-making parlance, a device used for making lures from lead or soft plastic. Molds can be made from plaster, aluminum alloy, or (in the case of soft plastic) hard rubber. They can be single (open) or two-piece, and, if the latter, pinned or hinged. *(See Hinged molds; Injection molds; Open molds; Pinned molds; Two-piece molds.)*

Neutral-base primer—A paint primer used on jigs and other lures molded of lead to neutralize the lead and prevent its oxidation.

Open mold—A mold made of plaster or hard rubber used in making plastic worms and other soft-bodied lures; also known as a "single-piece" mold. Open molds necessarily result in lures that are essentially flat on one side.

O'Shaughnessy—A popular hook style made from tempered (hard) steel and frequently used for spinnerbait construction. These hooks have forged (flattened) bends to further increase their strength; they usually break rather than bend.

Pin mold—A type of two-piece mold, the opposing halves of which are held in alignment by short steel posts called pins. *(See Hinged molds.)*

Plastisol—A viscous liquid plastic that solidifies when heated and then cooled. It is used for molding plastic (rubber) worms and other soft-bodied lures.

Power—A term used to describe the size of the line and lures for which a particular rod is designed. Power is usually quantified in terms ranging from "ultralight" to "extra heavy."

Reel—Once merely a device designed to hold line, reels have become integral parts of the fisherman's tackle system consisting of rod, reel, line, and terminal gear. The most popular reels in use today are spin-cast, spinning, casting, and fly, in that order.

Reel foot—The portion of a fishing reel that is affixed to the reel seat of the rod.

Reel seat—The portion of the handle assembly on a rod to which the reel is attached.

Reel-seat bushing—Cork, tape, or other material used to fill space between the rod blank and the reel seat.

Rod-wrapping jig—A device, either purchased or handmade, used to hold the rod blank securely as winding thread is wrapped on the blank to secure the guides or for decorative purposes.

Safety-pin spinnerbait—A type of spinnerbait, popular with southern bass fishermen, in which an integral shaft is bent in a configuration resembling that of a safety pin. The lower arm of the shaft contains a lead head and hook, while the upper arm accommodates one or two spinner blades, usually of Colorado design.

Scale netting—A small-mesh netting with hexagonal holes used to spray-paint realistic fish-scale patterns on lures. It is available in large and small sizes, differentiated by the size of the holes.

Screw eye—A wire loop having a pointed and partly threaded shaft, used in plug construction to affix hooks and line to the body of the lure. Screw eyes used for lure making are available in a variety of sizes and in open and closed configurations.

S-glass—A relatively new and superior type of fiberglass, developed in the 1970s, that is widely used in manufacturing quality rod blanks. S-glass has a tensile modulus about midway between that of E-glass and graphite. (*See Tensile modulus.*)

Single-strand leader wire—A highly tempered, stainless-steel wire developed for leader material, used in salt water and for toothed fish. In its heavier gauges, leader wire is used for making the shafts of spinnerbaits, and in its lighter gauges for making weed guards.

Slip sinker—Any of several sinker configurations having a center hole through which the fishing line is passed. Slip sinkers are favored because the fish is unable to detect their presence when picking up a plastic worm or live bait. Popular slip-sinker designs include egg, bullet, and Lindy or walking-sinker configurations.

Soft lead—Lead that has not been alloyed with tin or antimony; preferable for molding sinkers, jigs, and other molded lures.

Specie cork—A superior type of cork, favored for rod-handle construction because its pits run parallel to the center holes in cork rings, meaning that they will not be exposed as the handle is shaped. A cheaper, less desirable variety of cork, known as mustard cork, has pits that are at right angles to the center holes. (*See Cork rings.*)

Spine—In tackle-making parlance, the stiffest and more powerful side of a rod blank. Location of the spine is essential to proper guide placement.

Spinner blade—Any of several different varieties of slightly concave metal wafers used in the construction of spinnerbaits and sometimes in combination with live bait as fish attractors. There are at least a dozen blade configurations, about half of which are commonly used in lure construction.

Split ring—Concentric double spirals of spring steel that look like miniature key rings; used for a variety of fishing tackle applications, including affixing hooks to lures.

Split-ring pliers—Small, special-purpose pliers used to open split rings. These indispensable tools are characterized by having a tooth at the end of one jaw, which is forced between the opposing halves of the ring.

Sprue—In jig and other molded-lure construction, lead that has filled the sprue hole during pouring. Sprues are removed with side-cutter pliers or (preferably) by twisting until break-off occurs.

Sprue hole—The funnel-shaped hole in two-piece molds through which lead is poured into the main cavity or cavities of the mold.

Stirrup clevis—A type of clevis formed from round wire, the ends of which are flattened to receive drilled holes, through which a spinnerbait shaft is passed. Also known as a "wire" clevis. (*See Clevis; Folded clevis.*)

157

Tandem-blade spinnerbait—A modification of the safety-pin spinnerbait in which two spinner blades are hung from the upper arm, the forward blade being affixed to the shaft by a clevis.

Taper—An expression of how rapidly the diameter of a rod blank graduates from its tip to its butt. Taper influences the action and power of a rod.

Tenite—A tough plastic widely used in the manufacture of injection-molded lures. Most plastic lure bodies used by home tackle makers are made of this material.

Tensile modulus—The ability of a fiber to resist deformation and produce a high stiffness-to-weight ratio. It is the superior tensile modulus of graphite and boron that make them excellent materials for rod-blank construction.

Test—The numeric designation, expressed in pounds, of the tensile strength of a fishing line. Test is used to indicate the number of pounds of pull that can be exerted on wet line before breakage occurs.

Tiptop—The guide affixed to the tip of a fishing rod. It is mounted on a metal tube that is glued in place on the end of the rod.

Treble hook—A hook having three points, commonly used on plugs, spoons, and other lures.

Trim wrap—A short wrap applied to the rod blank immediately adjacent to the master wrap that holds the guide in place. Trim wraps are purely decorative. *(See Butt wrap; Master wrap; Underwrap.)*

Two-piece mold—A mold used for making lead and soft plastic lures in which the opposing halves are joined together by pins, hinges, clamps, or screws. An injection mold used to make plastic lures is a type of two-piece mold.

Underwrap—Winding thread wrapped on the rod blank as an underlay for butt wraps and for the guides and master wrap. Underwraps are used on heavy-duty rods to keep the guide feet from biting into the blank, and sometimes for decorative purposes on lighter rods.

Varnish—In tackle-making parlance, any of several formulations used to coat and protect winding thread after it has been wrapped on guides, lures, or whatever. Varnish is not applied to the blanks of modern (fiberglass, graphite, or boron) rods as it once was to bamboo rods.

Vinyl finish—A heavy-bodied, plastic-based paint used as a coating for jigs and other lead-bodied lures. Vinyl finish resists chipping better than enamel.

Weed guard—A short length of steel leader wire or fiber attached to the shank of a hook or the body of a jig to make them relatively snag-free. Weed guards should not extend past the point of a hook, lest they interfere with hooking ability.

Weedless hook—A hook made relatively snag-free by affixing a short length of wire or fiber to its shank. Virtually any hook can be made weedless.

Willowleaf blade—A type of spinner blade, popular for use with in-line spinnerbaits, in which the length of the blade is substantially greater than its width. The configuration, as the name implies, resembles that of a willow leaf.

Winding check—A small rubber or plastic washer seated on the rod blank immediately forward of the foregrip. It is considered a part of the handle assembly. *(See Hosel.)*

Windings—Spiral wraps of thread used to hold guides in place on a rod blank and also as decorations elsewhere on the blank; also known as wrappings. *(See Butt wrap; Diamond wrap; Guide wrap; Trim wrap.)*

Winding thread—Nylon thread used for wrapping guides on rods and for tying hair and other dressings on jigs and hooks. Winding thread is available in a variety of sizes and colors.

Hook Parts

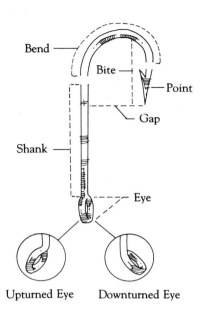

Bend

Bite

Point

Gap

Shank

Eye

Upturned Eye   Downturned Eye

Aberdeen Jig Hooks

Selected Hook Designs and Sizes

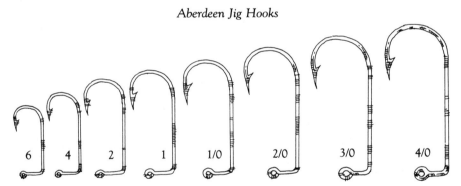

6   4   2   1   1/0   2/0   3/0   4/0

O'Shaughnessy Jig Hooks

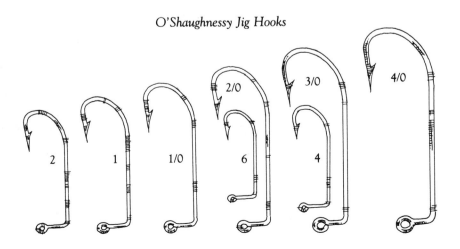

2   1   1/0   6   4   2/0   3/0   4/0

159

Treble Hooks

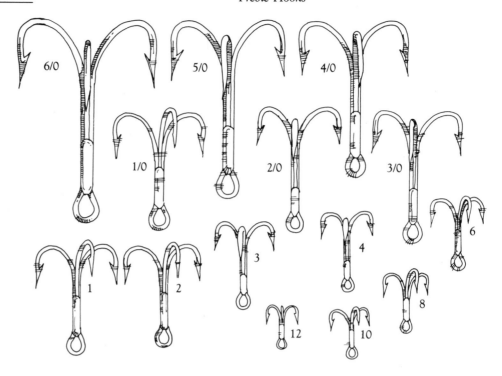

Round Bend Treble Hooks

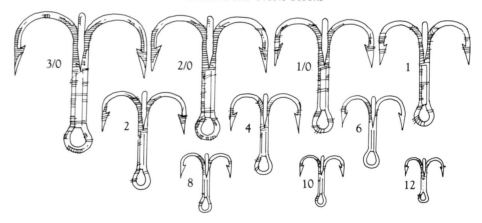

Double Hooks

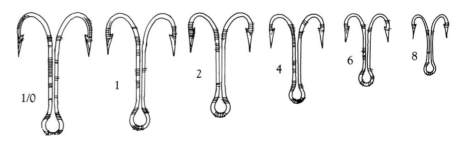

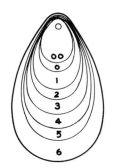 *Indiana*

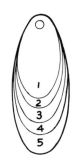 *Swing*

Spinner-Blade Designs and Sizes

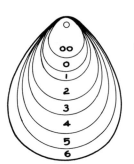 *Colorado*

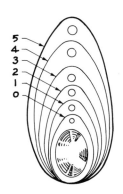 *French*

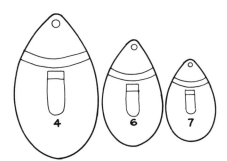

June-Bug

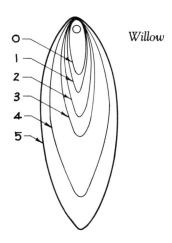 *Willow*

Fishing Knots You Should Know

Blood Knot

FOR JOINING LINES OF DIFFERENT DIAMETER

Double Fisherman

FOR JOINING LINES OF EQUAL DIAMETER

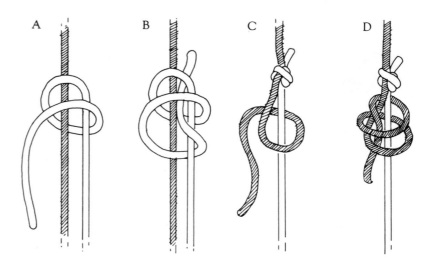

Palomar

FOR ATTACHING LINE TO HOOK

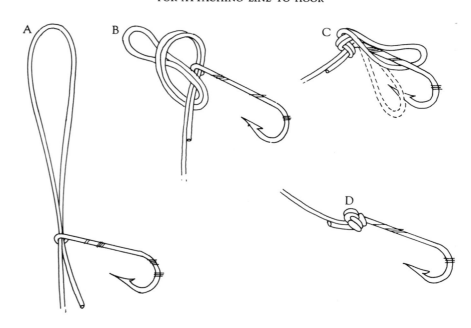

162

Arbor Knot
FOR ATTACHING LINE TO REEL

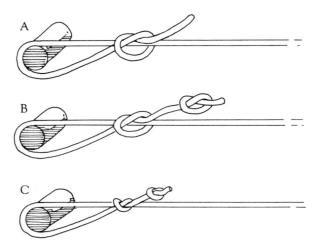

Bowline
FOR MAKING A LOOP IN END OF LINE

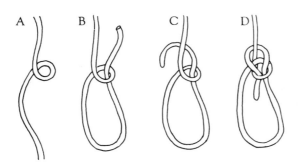

Improved Clinch Knot
FOR ATTACHING LINE TO HOOK OR LURE

Basic

Twice through Eye

Appendix B. Where to Order What You Need

Here is a list of several major tackle supply houses, followed—in italics—by the items in which they specialize. It includes only those suppliers that the author can personally recommend and is not intended to be a comprehensive list. Two excellent sources for workbench tools are also listed.

THE ANGLER'S SUPPLY HOUSE
P.O. Box 996
Williamsport, PA 17703
(717) 323-7564

Visa and MasterCard accepted.
Fly-tying kits and supplies, hooks, swivels and snaps, jig molds, spinner blades, spinnerbait beads and bodies, plastic plug bodies, rod blanks and components.

ANGLER'S WORKSHOP
P.O. Box 1044
Woodland, WA 98674
(206) 225-6359

Visa and MasterCard accepted.
Rod blanks and components (Lamiglas, Fenwick, and Sage blanks; Fuji and Perfection guides and tiptops), rod-building accessories.

BASS PRO SHOPS
P.O. Box 4046
Springfield, MO 65808
Toll-free orders: 1-800-227-7776

Visa and MasterCard accepted.
Bass Pro Shops specializes in a broad selection of ready-made tackle, boats, clothing, and outdoor equipment. For the do-it-yourselfer, they also offer fly-tying supplies, spinnerbait components, worm-making supplies, jig molds and lead-melting equipment, hooks, rubber skirts, and a limited selection of rod-building components.

BROOKSTONE
127 Vose Farm Road
Peterborough, NH 03458
(603) 924-9511

American Express, Visa, and MasterCard accepted.
Outstanding (if expensive) selection of hard-to-find workbench tools, including miniature tools that are helpful for many tackle-making chores.

CABELA'S
812 13th Avenue
Sidney, NB 69160
Toll-free orders (credit card only): 1-800-237-4444
Customer Service: 1-800-237-8888

Visa and MasterCard accepted.
A broad selection of ready-made tackle, boating equipment, and outdoor supplies. For the do-it-yourselfer, they offer an excellent line of house-brand and Fenwick rod-building supplies and accessories, workbench items, fly-tying supplies, spinnerbait components, terminal gear, Mustad and Eagle Claw hooks, and jig-making molds and accessories.

DALE CLEMENS CUSTOM TACKLE INC.
444 Schantz Spring Road
Allentown, PA 18104
(215) 395-5119

Outstanding selection of rod-building components and supplies, including Fenwick, Lamiglas, Shakespeare, and Custom Builder (house-brand) blanks; Fuji, Mildrum, and Aftco guides and tiptops; and a wide selection of reel seats and handles. Also, a good selection of fly-tying supplies and tools, and a modest selection of jig-making molds and ready-made jig heads. (The Clemens catalog contains rod-building instructions that are most comprehensive.)

LURE-CRAFT INDUSTRIES, INC.
P.O. Box 35
Solsberry, IN 47459
(812) 825-9088

The place to go for rubber-worm supplies—molds, liquid plastic, color additive, hot pots, pouring pans, etc. A limited selection of jig and safety-pin spinnerbait bodies, hooks, and fly-tying accessories is also available.

THE NETCRAFT COMPANY
2800 Tremainsville Road
Toledo, OH 43613
(419) 472-9826

Visa and MasterCard accepted ($5 minimum order).
Probably the nation's best selection of net and seine-making supplies. Also, a wide choice of hooks, lure-making equipment and supplies (including tenite lure bodies), spinner blades, beads, and spinnerbait bodies; paints and cements (including an excellent airbrush set for $11.95); aluminum molds; plastic and rubber skirts; fly-tying materials; wire-bending devices; and a limited choice of rod-making components.

PFEIFFER'S TACKLE CRAFTERS
14303 Robcaste Road
Phoenix, MD 21131
(301) 667-6464 (office)
(301) 472-2555 (warehouse)

Visa and MasterCard preferred.
A truly outstanding selection of rod-making components, tools, and supplies, including Loomis boron and graphite blanks; Fenwick, Lamiglas, Dynaflex, and Shakespeare (including Ugly Stik) blanks; Aetna, Fuji, Aftco, and Perfection guides and tiptops; Gudebrod products; Aftco, Fuji, Rodon, and Varmac handles and reel seats; and a variety of preformed and ring-cork handles. Also a modest selection of spinnerbait components, aluminum molds and accessories, worm molds, and liquid plastic.

REED TACKLE
P.O. Box 1348
Fairfield, NJ 07007
(201) 227-0409

Visa and MasterCard accepted.
Fly-tying materials; a wide selection of hooks for all purposes; Aetna and Mildarbide guides; proprietary (Reed-Flex) glass and graphite rod blanks; a modest selection of rod handles; spinner blades in a variety of sizes and styles; stainless-steel leader wire; and preformed jig heads.

SHOFF TACKLE SUPPLY
405 West Gowe Street
P.O. Box 1227
Kent, WA 98032
(206) 852-7304

Visa and MasterCard accepted.
Good selection of rod blanks and rod-building accessories, including Fenwick, Lamiglas, and Sage blanks; Hypalon and cork grips and handles; Fuji casting and spinning handles; Shoff and Varmac reel seats; and Aetna guides and tiptops. Also, Gudebrod products, varnish, color preservative, and an excellent (if somewhat expensive) rod-winding jig.

SPORTSMAN'S SUPPLIES
2924 South Avenue
Toledo, OH 43609
(419) 381-9777

Visa and MasterCard accepted.
A good, all-around selection of tackle-making supplies, including Fenwick and G. Loomis rod blanks, Fenwick and Fuji handles, Fuji guides and tiptops; a good assortment of spinner blades and other spinnerbait components (including delta blades and aluminum rivets for buzzbaits); plastic lure bodies and scale masking; living rubber skirts; spinnerbait heads; aluminum molds; a good choice of Mustad and Eagle Claw hooks; and a limited selection of fly-tying supplies.

TACKLE CHANDLERS
P.O. Box 3041
Wilmington, DE 19804
(303) 998-7584

Visa and MasterCard accepted.
A comprehensive selection of rod-making supplies, tools, and accessories, including Lamiglas rod kits and blanks; Shakespeare boron, graphite, and Ugly Stik blanks; J. Kennedy Fisher glass and graphite blanks; and Lew Childre "speed-glass" blanks. Also, Fuji and Ken Wiebe handles; Fuji and Aftco reel seats; Aetna, Aftco, Fuji, Mildrum, and Perfection guides and tiptops; Gudebrod products; and a good choice of rod-building tools and workbench equipment.

WOODCRAFT
41 Atlantic Avenue
P.O. Box 4000
Woburn, MA 01888
Toll-free orders: 1-800-225-1153

American Express, Visa, and MasterCard accepted.
An outstanding collection of workbench and woodworking tools, many of which will prove helpful to tackle makers. Included are whittler's knives, brass hammers, gouges, needle files and rasps, power carving tools, bench-top lathes, and much more.

Index

169